REMEMBER NATIVE AMERICA!

The Earthworks of Ancient America

REMEMBER NATIVE AMERICA!

The Earthworks of Ancient America

Five Flower Press

Santa Fe, New Mexico

035001

BY RICHARD BALTHAZAR

Publisher's Cataloging in Publication
(Prepared by Quality Books Inc.)

Balthazar, Richard.
Remember native America! : the earthworks of ancient America /Richard Balthazar.
p.   cm.
Includes bibliographical references.
ISBN 0-9632661-0-1

1. Indians of North America—United States—History.
2. Indians of North America—United States—Art.
I. Title.

E77.B3 1992   997
              QB192-616

Editorial Assistance: Ernesto Torres and Ione Caley
Design/Typography: John Cole Graphic Designer, Cerrillos, NM
    Software used to produce this publication: Quark XPress 3.1,
    Adobe Photoshop 2.01, Adobe Streamline 1.0 and Adobe Illustrator 3.0.
Typeface: Adobe Cochin
Printing: Inland Press

Printed on acid free paper

ACKNOWLEDGEMENTS

Sincere gratitude to Ernesto Torres for his superb work in editing the text of this album; to Ione Caley for her unerring eye for consistency; to John Cole for his artistry and expertise in its design and production; to Joe Stuart for some very valuable advice; and to the Western States Arts Federation (WESTAF) for providing time to undertake this labor of love.

Front cover illustration:
ROGAN PLATE #1
Repoussé copper with cutouts
AD 1200 - 1400
Etowah, Bartow County, Georgia
Location unknown.

This figure is the finest example of the Mississippian Falcon Warrior with typical wings, ceremonial mace, headdress, apron-pouch, beaded forelock, and seashell pendant. The original has suffered damage to the feet and some central portions.

Back cover illustration:
ORNAMENT
Beaten copper
100 BC - AD 100, Ohio
Location unknown

Native copper, widely available around the Great Lakes area, was the precious metal of the Native Americans of North America throughout their history. Lacking knowledge of smelting or casting processes, they cold-hammered the copper for personal and ceremonial ornamentation.

This work is dedicated to the memory of the multitudes who peopled America for thousands of years before the arrival of Columbus.

Lamenting the holocaust that followed upon this pivotal event, now five hundred years later, I offer these images from the ancient heritage of the Native American world.

CONTENTS

▲▼▲

IN THE EARLY NINETEEN SEVENTIES when the District of Columbia was in the throes of urban renewal, I was one of the foolhardy types called urban pioneers. Owner of a large Victorian house in the heart of the slum, I lived for seven years in the only habitable house on a block I jokingly christened Desolation Row.

Also owner of a large blue van, I was reckless enough to engage in salvaging architectural details from many nearby houses slated to be renewed.

Illustration: CLAW—Mica cutout, 28 X 17 cm
100 BC - AD 100, Hopewell Mound, Ross County, Ohio
Ohio Historical Society

A material frequent in ornamentation ornamentation was sheet mica cut into figures and designs. Large caches of mica were found with burials, indicating its precious nature.

Scrambling around in derelict buildings, often with stairways collapsed or burnt out, I felt outraged that the painstaking handiwork of our forefathers was being destroyed. Even moreso when I witnessed a public library falling to the wrecking ball — replete with books on shelves. From then on I felt simply no compunction about saving what I personally could and stored it in my half-demolished basement. A couple of the many mantles fit well in my house while the rest of it, woodwork, brass fittings, plasterwork details, and so on, eventually was passed on to fellow pioneers in the Logan Circle Historic District.

Thanks to a chance discovery made during this pioneering period of my life, I can now offer this book, *Remember Native America*! On 12th Street Northwest stood a lovely Grecian Revival building with white Doric columns. Long the home of a black Masonic lodge, it got in the way of a modern city project. The secret brotherhood fled elsewhere, abandoning their library to the bulldozers. Having spied these several hundred books through a shattered window, I enlisted the aid of like-minded neighbors to quickly box and spirit them away.

For the next two years, these cartons served well as a platform for a guest mattress. One day, enjoying a rare respite from the neverending process of restoring my house, I pulled one of the boxes out for something to read. I flipped through a lot of nineteenth century pulp novels until, at the very bottom of the box, I came upon a large tome with fancy leather binding — *Ancient Monuments of the Mississippi Valley*, by E. G. Squier and E. H. Davis.

From 1848 as the first of the Smithsonian Contributions to Knowledge, the book both described and provided detailed surveys of magnificent earthworks and mounds discovered by early settlers, primarily in Ohio. I had never heard even a whisper about any of this during all my too many years of schooling. My curiosity definitely piqued, I began investigating the moundbuilders, as these pre-Columbian Native Americans of the eastern half of the United States were called.

In the eighteenth and early nineteenth centuries, countless prehistoric earthworks were discovered in the course of the first western encroachments by settlers from the new United States of America. By the mid nineteenth century, as the expanding nation spilled into its new territories to and beyond the Mississippi River, the earthworks of the mysterious moundbuilders were found everywhere. The fascinated public subscribed to several myths, including theories about Atlantis and the Lost Tribes of Israel. The central Mississippi River valley was popularly viewed as America's Egypt. Towns were named Cairo, Karnak, Memphis, Alexandria, and featured prominent Mound streets, avenues, cemeteries, parks, and lakes.

The 1890-91 Annual Report of the Smithsonian Institution's Bureau of Ethnology was devoted to the monumental (742 pages) *Report on the Mound Explorations* by Cyrus Thomas. This work, an authoritative compendium of hundreds of mound sites across the new country, was the result of great public interest which, however, even then was already beginning to change dramatically. Because of the Indian Wars, public attitudes were less than receptive to subjects that lent legitimacy to Native American claims to the lands being appropriated in fulfillment of the new nation's Manifest Destiny.

By the turn of the century, Americans had mostly forgotten the moundbuilders. Fortunately, the academic community of archaeologists and anthropologists continued to explore and document this vast heritage of Native America. Unfortunately, their serious work and marvelous discoveries have received far too little public attention.

Compounding these factors was plain human nature. By the turn of the century, treasure-hunters had ransacked most of the ancient local landmarks. Huge quantities of artifacts disappeared into private collections. Though this was by and large the rule, many barrels of relics were dutifully sent to the Smithsonian for safekeeping. Over the years, many more earthworks fell to the plow in farmers' fields or were leveled for a town's new streets and neighborhoods. Thus thousands of earthworks and moundbuilder artifacts vanished forever.

What little remains cannot compare with what once existed. Yet what remains at protected sites reveals the magnificence of moundbuilder artistry. Through these earthworks, we can catch fleeting glimpses of that Native American world of the past.

Now is a rightful and overdue time to remember Native America!

This book is conceived not as scholarly documentation, but as an album of images including surveys and maps from Squier and Davis, Thomas, (indicated respectively by S- and T- with the illustration numbers) and others, as well as some of my own photographs and line-drawings of artifacts. These black and white images will provide a visual journey through the more than three thousand years of Native American history before Columbus came to the New World. For you, may it truly be a journey of discovery!

1.

DISTRIBUTION OF EARTHWORKS
IN THE EASTERN UNITED STATES

Native American earthworks have been
found over a vast area extending into
some 20 present-day states and two
Canadian provinces. This range corre-
sponds most closely to the geographical
area called the Eastern Woodlands, as
opposed to the Great Plains, the Desert
Southwest, and so on. Shadings on the
map indicate frequency of the earthworks, which are of various types and
from three distinct eras.

1.

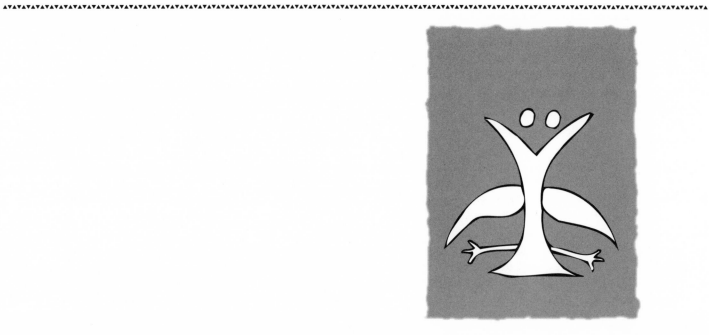

NATIVE AMERICAN HISTORY EXTENDS into the depths of past millenia. Throughout the hemisphere, primordial bands of hunter-gatherers wandered more than ten thousand years ago. As early as 3000 BC, throughout the Ohio River drainage and northeast into New England, lived a people of whom all we know is a burial rite of staining their corpses with red ochre, a hallmark of

Illustration: BIRD MOTIF—Incised design on stone pendant, red jasper, 8.65 X 2.9 cm diameter
Poverty Point culture, ca. 1200 BC, Northeastern Louisiana
Thomas Gilcrease Institute of American History and Art

This bird design is the first appearance of a theme traceable throughout the history of Native America. The ancient people who created it made no ceramics other than baked clay balls which they heated and used in watertight baskets to cook. Only these and small stone items such as this pendant have been found.

Neolithic cultures in many parts of the world. Thus they are called the Red Ochre culture.

By 1500 BC the Red Ochre peoples around the Great Lakes began burying their dead in the small knolls *(kames)* left by the melting glaciers. For this they became known as the Glacial Kame culture. Within a few centuries there arose a new tradition of burial in artificial mounds of earth. By the end of the era these people, the Adena, who were named for a site in the valley of the Scioto River in south central Ohio, had spread over a large area in the upper drainage of the Ohio River.

Meanwhile, around 1500 BC in northern Louisiana along Bayou Macon (perhaps then a lower channel of the Arkansas River), another moundbuilding culture arose. Now Poverty Point State Commemorative Area, the site was a complex of large ceremonial earthworks and living areas surrounding a plaza of 37 acres. This culture might well be called "Arkansas" for its river location as well as the area it encompassed, including parts of present-day Arkansas and Mississippi.

Construction of their spectacular Bird Mound began by 1500 BC. It was completed by 1200 BC as the civilization reached its classic stage. Thus the Arkansas peoples lived earlier than the Olmec of Mexico (classic by 900 BC), long reputed to be the New World's first native civilization.

(For the record, that honor actually belongs to a nameless South American people in Peru, 2000 - 1500 BC, who cultivated the bean and built dozens of complexes of stone-walled rooms around a temple/warehouse. Their principal site, El Paraíso, would be a good name for this earliest Native American civilization. See Reading List: Engel.)

For a thousand years the Arkansas peoples lived in their city of several thousand at Poverty Point and in many towns such as the Jaketown site in Mississippi and the Deep Bayou site in Arkansas. Several of the regional centers also incorporated embankments and heaped mounds (not for burial) in their design. Supply routes for various stone materials extended to the Ozark Mountains, Lake Michigan, and the Tennessee River valley.

The Arkansas people for some reason simply disappeared between 700 and 600 BC.

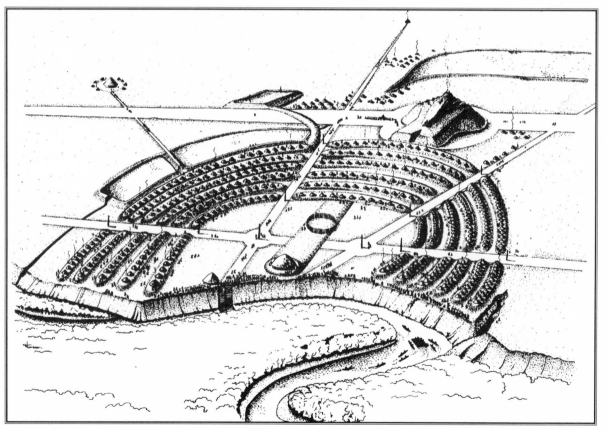

2.

POVERTY POINT, WEST CARROLL PARISH, LOUISIANA (1500 - 600 BC)

The Bird Mound, which rises to 70 feet, is now scarcely so distinct. The concentric house mounds are barely detectable. The ring of posts on the plaza may have been used for astronomical observations; the embanked square in the background may have been for a sport. Poverty Point is presently a State Commemorative Area. Drawing by Jon L. Gibson.

2.

▲▽

SURVIVING WELL BEYOND THE END OF the Archaic Period, the Adena of Ohio, who built conical burial mounds, continued to occupy the river basin. By 400 to 300 BC, however, there arose among them new traits which anthropologists call the Hopewell Cult of the Woodland Tradition.

The Hopewell, a new genetic type with long skulls, apparently established dominion in some way over the round-headed Adena population, but soon adopted much of the native culture, including reverence for the bird and the ritual of mound burial. However, with the Hopewell came new earth-working traditions. By 100 BC there were large ceremonial centers along the valley of the Scioto and other rivers in southern Ohio which incorporated

Illustration: HUMAN HEAD EFFIGY PIPE —Stone, 100 BC - AD 100, Ohio, Dimensions and location unknown

A woodcut from Squier and Davis.

embanked circles, squares, and octagons, as well as many hillforts. (Nearly all the earthworks pictured on the following pages have now disappeared, though their present condition is given when known.)

For several centuries the Hopewell flourished. Through vast trading connections across the eastern half of the country, they obtained valuable minerals from as far away as Wyoming and seashell from the Gulf Coast. Everywhere a trade link was established, mound building spread, and societies began to take root, including among numerous others, Crystal River in Florida, Marksville in Louisiana, the Copena on the Tennessee River, the Kansas City Hopewell on the Missouri, the Havana Hopewell on the Illinois, and the Effigy Mound peoples of Iowa and Wisconsin.

Soon after AD 300 the Ohio world began to decline. For some unknown reason, most of the population of the heartland had vanished by AD 500. But in other areas, the societies with whom they traded lived on to come into their own.

S-3.

GREAT MOUND AT GRAVE CREEK, MARSHALL COUNTY, WEST VIRGINIA

This burial mound was originally 70 feet high, but early excavations have left it much reduced. Two burial chambers were found, one at the base and another 30 feet above. In the lower were two skeletons; in the upper was one, with thousands of shell beads, mica ornaments, copper bracelets, and various stone articles. It now sits in Grave Creek Mound State Park in the town of Moundville.

S-3.

S-4.
GREAT MOUND, MARIETTA,
WASHINGTON COUNTY,
OHIO

This burial mound has been preserved in the Marietta cemetery
since the town was first settled,
but the surrounding embankment
is now much less noticeable than
in the picture.

5.
BURIAL MOUND, WASHING-
TON COUNTY, OHIO

Of a more modest and usual size
is this burial mound which sits in
a cornfield along the Muskingum
River, having survived some two
thousand years. While hundreds
of such have vanished, many more
remain in the eastern half of the
United States, but they too often
are only a minor footnote in local
folklore.

S-4.

5.

6.
GREAT MOUND,
MIAMISBURG, MONTGOMERY
COUNTY, OHIO

This burial mound perches on the
highest hill in the area just above
a golf course. When excavated, a
burial was found some twenty feet
down. A chamber at the base was
empty.

6.

S-7.

NEWARK WORKS, LICKING
COUNTY, OHIO

One of the largest Ohio earthworks
covering more than four square
miles, this work contains most of
the classical forms of Hopewell
earthworking, including squares and
circles of various sizes and long parallel embankments creating avenues.
These have now been substantially
obliterated by the modern town.

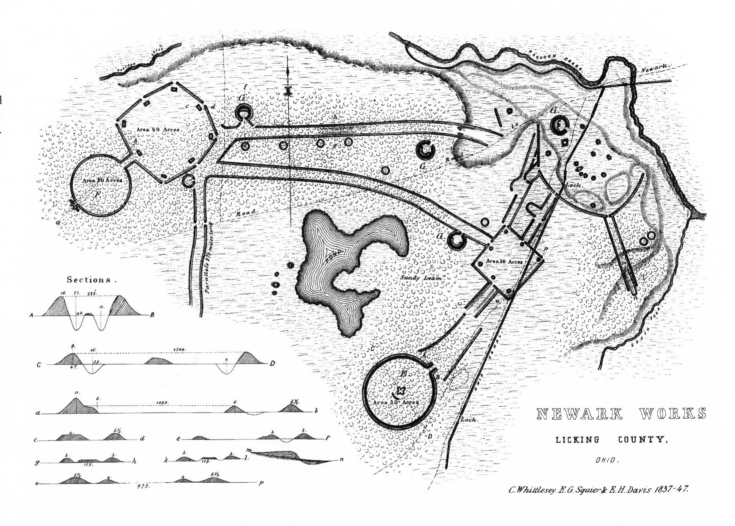

NEWARK WORKS

LICKING COUNTY,

OHIO.

C.Whittlesey. E.G.Squier & E.H.Davis 1837-47.

S-7.

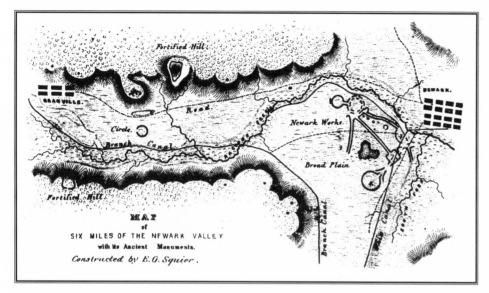

S-8.

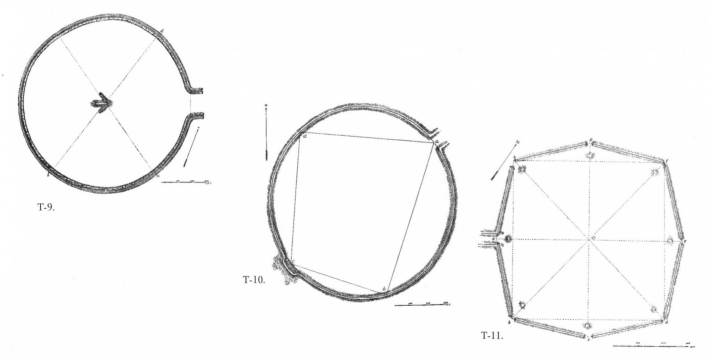

T-9.

T-10.

T-11.

S-8.
SIX MILES OF THE
NEWARK VALLEY

"But a small proportion of the mounds occurring within this range are shown on this map." —*Squier.* Note the varied earthworks in the vicinity of the Newark Works.

T-9.
FAIR GROUND CIRCLE, NEWARK

The Great Circle is now in a lovely park with a museum. Note the bird mound in the center. The Circle's walls are several feet high and enclose an interior moat.

T-10.
OBSERVATORY CIRCLE, NEWARK

This perfect circle (2,880 feet in circumference) and the Octagon below are now in a golf course. Opposite the entrance is a feature 8 feet higher than the embankment overlooking the enclosure.

T-11.
OCTAGON, NEWARK

In area 50+ acres, the Octagon has openings at each angle with gateway mounds shielding each entrance.

S-12.
TARLTON CROSS,
PICKAWAY COUNTY, OHIO

The work is 90 feet across and 3 feet high; in the center is a circular depression 20 feet across. The sides of the cross correspond to the cardinal points. "Several small mounds occur nearby; and upon the high hill, a spur of which is occupied by the cross, are several huge mounds." —*Squier*.

The cross is now thickly wooded over.

S-13.
ALLIGATOR,
LICKING COUNTY, OHIO

Called such in the time of Squier and Davis, this effigy mound looks more like an opossum, considering the tail and well-defined head. Located not far from the Newark Works on a hill approximately 200 feet high, it is 250 feet long. The head, shoulders, and rump are more elevated than other parts. The circular space behind the body was covered with burned stones.

S-14.
ROCK MILL WORK,
FAIRFIELD COUNTY, OHIO

Occupying the top of a 200-foot hill, this work consisted of a square (420 feet on a side), two circles, and a mound which "overlooks every part and commands a wide prospect on every hand." —*Squier*

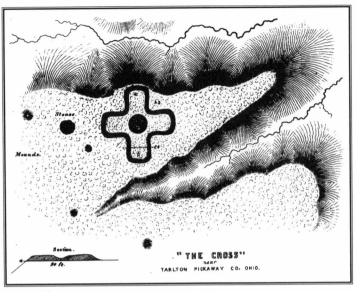

S-12.

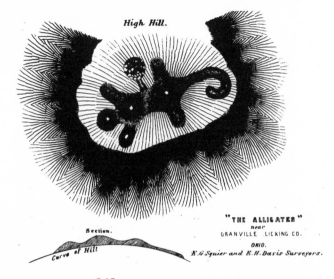

S-13.

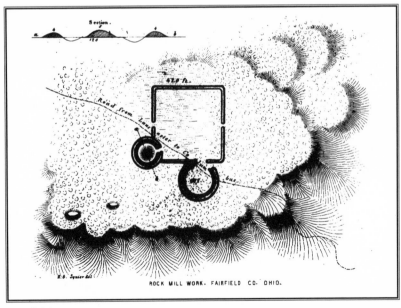

S-14.

S-15.
PORTSMOUTH WORKS,
SCIOTO COUNTY, OHIO
AND GREENUP COUNTY,
KENTUCKY

This work extended some eight miles along both banks of the Ohio River at the mouth of the Scioto. The town of Portsmouth now covers most of the Ohio section. Particularly remarkable is the several-miles-long avenue of parallel lines, about 4 feet high and 160 feet apart, which align on both sides of the Ohio River.

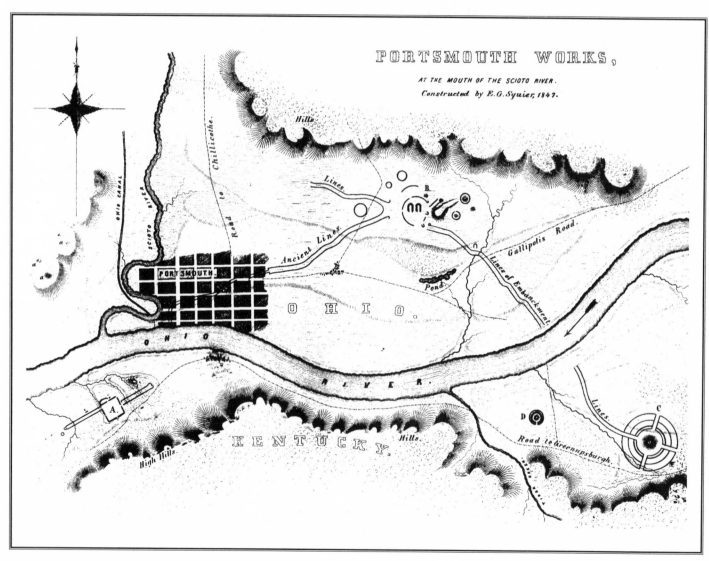

PORTSMOUTH WORKS,
AT THE MOUTH OF THE SCIOTO RIVER.
Constructed by E.G. Squier, 1847.

S-15.

S-16.
DETAILS OF PORTSMOUTH WORKS

Group A: Kentucky shore. The 800-foot square is exact with walls about 12 feet high. The avenues are both 2,100 feet long. Group B: Ohio shore. Group C: Kentucky shore. The four avenues to the central mound conform very nearly to the cardinal points. A graded way led up to the mound's flat top.

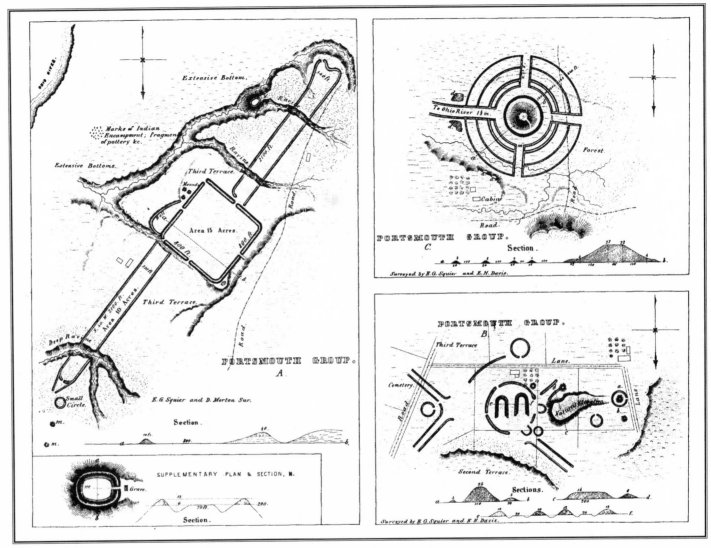

S-16.

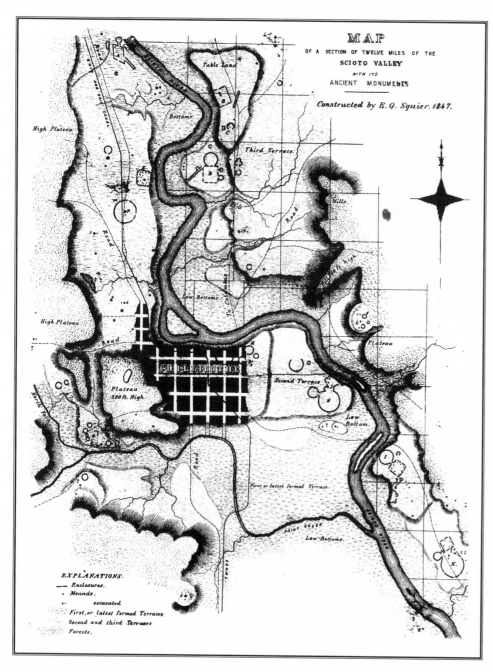

S-17.

S-17.
MAP OF THE SCIOTO VALLEY

There were no fewer than ten groups of large works accompanied by mounds of various sizes in the vicinity of Chillicothe. Mound City Group National Monument is near the river in the upper left. The Hopeton works are immediately across the river. Several more geometrical earthworks were located along the Paint Creek beyond the map at the lower left.

S-18.

PAINT CREEK WORKS,
ROSS COUNTY, OHIO

No. 1: 14 miles from Chillicothe. Once the best preserved work in the valley, it has now been plowed down.

No. 2: The large elliptical mound near the center is now known as Seip Mound and is all that remains in a small park surrounded by plowed fields.

No. 3: One mile south of Chillicothe. This earthwork was under cultivation by 1800.

No. 4: Near Frankfort. All that remains of this work is one mound near a roadway.

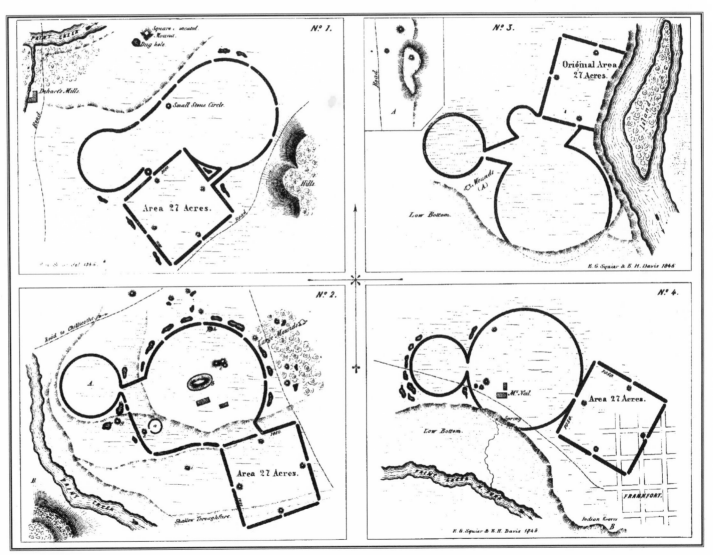

S-18.

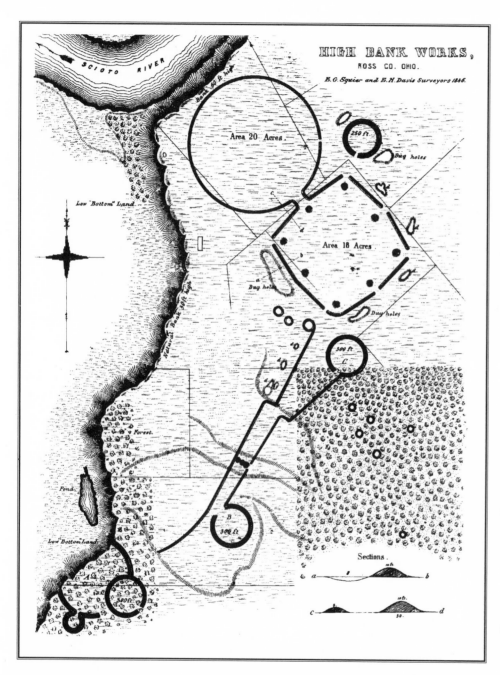

HIGH BANK WORKS,
ROSS CO. OHIO.
E.G. Squier and E.H. Davis Surveyors 1846.

SCIOTO RIVER

Area 20 Acres

250 ft

Dug holes

Low "Bottom" Land

Area 18 Acres

Dug holes

Dug holes

300 ft
C

Forest

Pond

Low Bottom Land

B
300 ft

Sections

a   b
c   d

300 ft

S-19.

S-19.
HIGH BANK WORKS,
ROSS COUNTY, OHIO

Five miles below Chillicothe. The
octagon measured 950 feet in diameter; the circle 1,050 feet. The walls of
the octagon were between 11 and 12
feet high. The smaller circles are some
300 feet in diameter and, as in many
of the works, have moats inside the
embanked walls.

S-20.
HOPETON WORKS,
ROSS COUNTY, OHIO

The rectangle measured 950 X 900
feet; the circle was 1,050 feet in diameter. The works are presently on private land and have almost disappeared.

S-21.
LIBERTY WORKS,
ROSS COUNTY, OHIO

Eight miles southeast of Chillicothe.
The walls were no more than 4 feet
high; the square was 1,080 feet per
side with gateways 30 feet wide; the
circle at 1,700 feet in diameter was
one of the largest.

S-22.
ANCIENT WORK,
PIKE COUNTY, OHIO

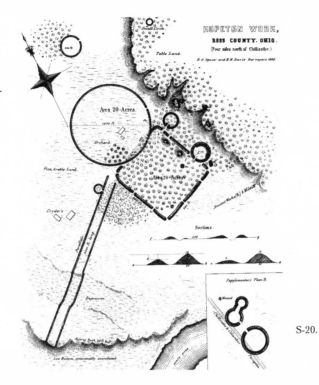

S-20.

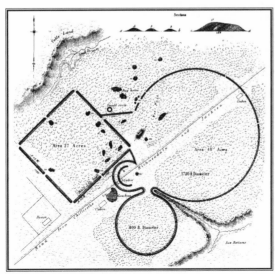

S-21.

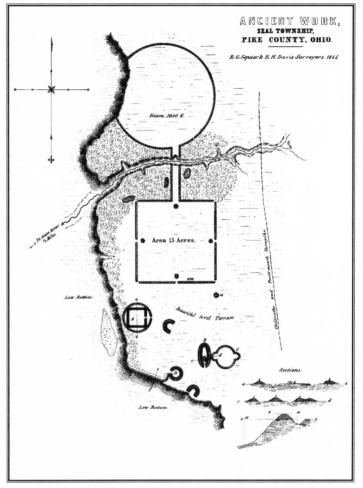

S-22.

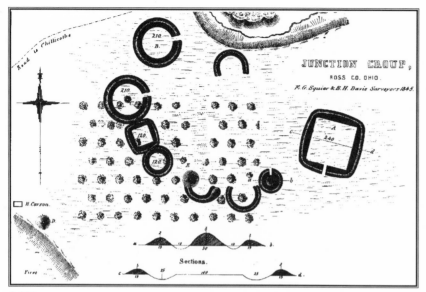

S-23A.

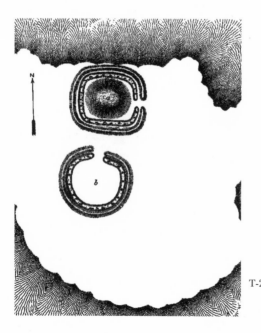

T-24.

S-23B.

S-23.
JUNCTION AND
BLACKWATER GROUPS,
ROSS COUNTY, OHIO

These works are the best examples
of a type of figure with interior moat
which was in all likelihood residen-
tial in function. Figures without
entrances to the interior platforms
are puzzling given this context.

T-24.
WORKS ON THE DAVIS
PLACE, HOCKING COUNTY,
OHIO

The Works sit atop a 200-foot bluff.
The 23-foot mound contained a log
burial vault.

S-25.
MARIETTA WORKS, MARIET-
TA, WASHINGTON COUNTY,
OHIO

The survey also shows the layout of
the town. All that remains of the
earthworks is 1) the Great Mound at
lower right; 2) Platform A in a park;
3) Platform B under a public library;
and 4) the Graded Way which is now
a street leading to the river. These
works will be mentioned again since
Marietta was also inhabited in the
following era.

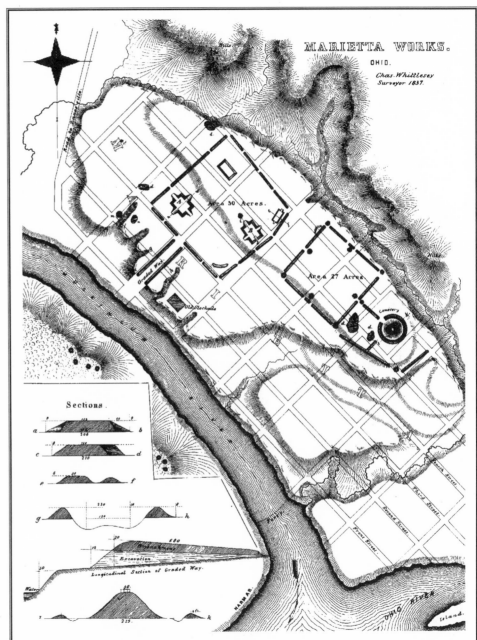

S-25.

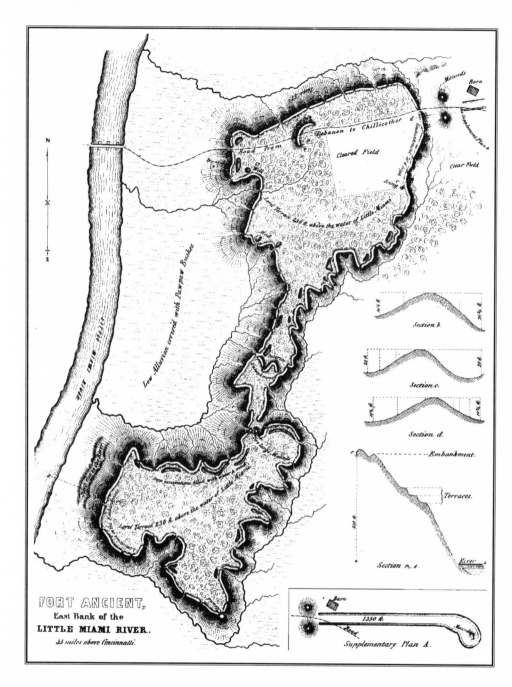

S-26.
FORT ANCIENT,
WARREN COUNTY, OHIO

Southwest of their Scioto heartland,
the Hopewell constructed fortified
hilltops, probably as a line of defense
against other peoples. The forts were
frequently of such a size that entire
populations could have lived or taken
shelter within. Among the almost
4 miles of embankments at Fort
Ancient, which rise at points to as
much as 20 feet, are over 70 gateways. The site is now a State Memorial.

S-26.

S-27.
FORT HILL,
HIGHLAND COUNTY, OHIO

Located on a 500-foot hill, the wall is 8,224 feet long and varies from 6 to 15 feet in height. Fort Hill is a State Memorial.

S-28.
FORTIFIED HILL,
BUTLER COUNTY, OHIO

Constructed on a 250-foot hill, the walls are about 5 feet high. Note the complexly embanked gateways.

S-27.

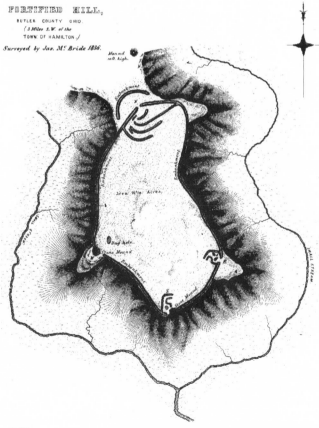

S-28.

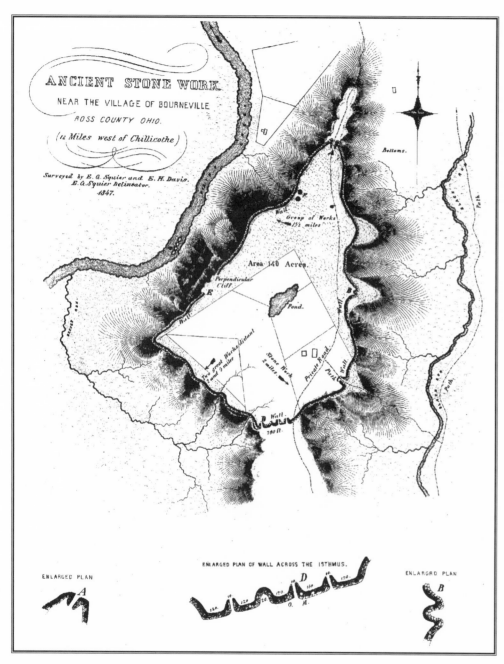

S-29.
ANCIENT STONE WORK
NEAR BOURNEVILLE,
ROSS COUNTY, OHIO

Now known as Spruce Hill, this work is rare in Ohio because of its stone construction. Such stone forts have also been found in Kentucky and Tennessee, the southern Hopewell frontier. This work is presently on private land.

30.
OLD STONE FORT,
MANCHESTER, COFFEE
COUNTY, TENNESSEE

Perched above Duck River, heaped stone and earth walls combine with 85-foot cliffs to extend 1 and 1/4 miles around 50 acres. Site map courtesy Old Stone Fort State Archaeological Area, from a source cited as "Jones, 1876."

30.

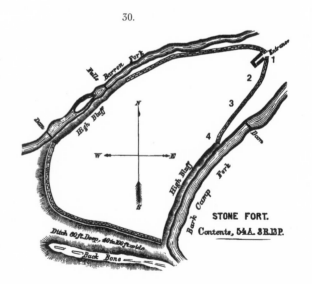

S-31.
SERPENT, ADAMS COUNTY, OHIO

The most famous earthwork in the Americas and the world's largest manifestation of the subject, this fabulous Serpent effigy mound lies on a 150-foot-high spur and is some 1400 feet in length and 4 to 5 feet in height. It is usually interpreted as a snake about to swallow an egg (i.e., the cosmos). A circular pile of burnt stones, perhaps an altar, once lay in the center of the oval. The survey shows triangular elevations near the head which have not been noted in later renderings. These triangles suggest connections with the uniquely American symbology of the plumed serpent. If so, this would also be among the earliest of its representations. The Serpent is now a State Memorial and has been somewhat altered.

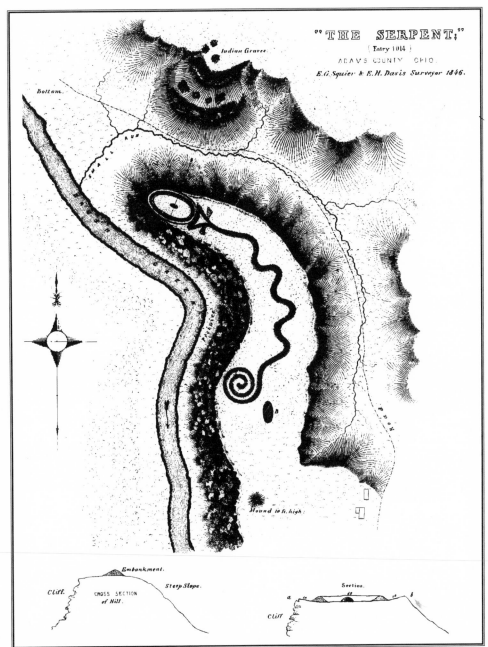

S-31.

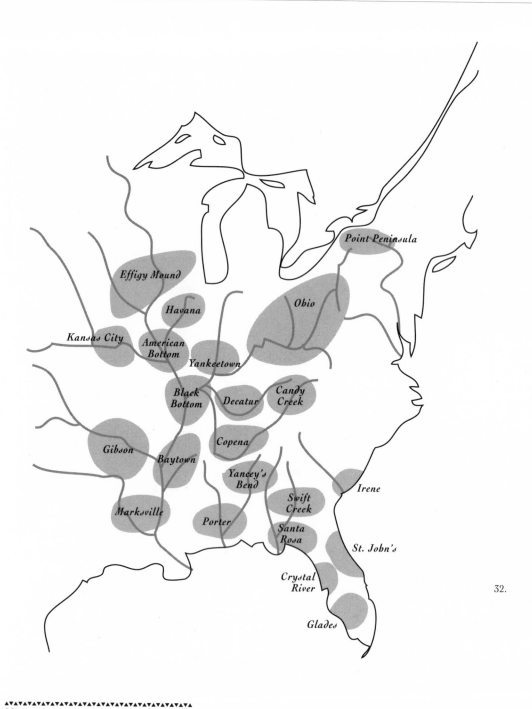

32.

LATE OHIO AREA AND
NEIGHBORING PEOPLES
(AD 100 - 500)

While the traditions of Hopewell
geometric earthworks were mostly
practiced in the southern half of present-day Ohio, occasionally the construction of figurative earthworks
with interior moats and, more frequently, the practice of mound burial
spread to contact societies in West
Virginia, western Pennsylvania, New
York, Michigan, Kentucky, and
across Illinois into Missouri and
Iowa, as well as throughout the
Southeast into Florida.

32.

T-33.

GROUP NEAR CHARLESTON, KANAWHA COUNTY, WEST VIRGINIA

The works consisted of 50 mounds 3 to 35 feet in height and 8 to 10 enclosures of 1 to 30 acres, with evidence of house sites.

T-34.

MOUND NO. 1 AND ENCLOSURE *A*, NEAR CHARLESTON

The enclosure was 556 feet in circumference, 3 feet high; the mound inside was also 3 feet high. Mound No. 1, known locally as the Criel mound, was 33 feet high with a leveled top 40 feet across. "The top was leveled in order to erect thereon an office and judges' stand in connection with a racecourse about it."
—*Thomas.*

T-35. ENCLOSURE G, NEAR CHARLESTON

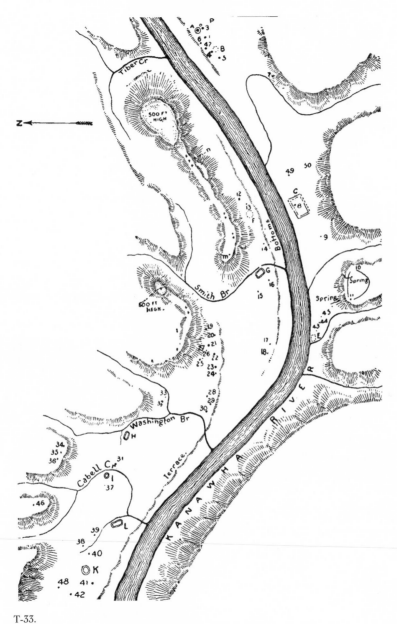

T-33.

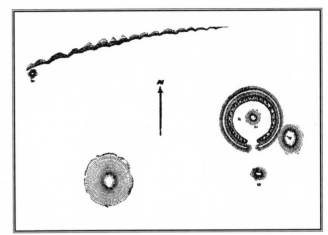

T-34.

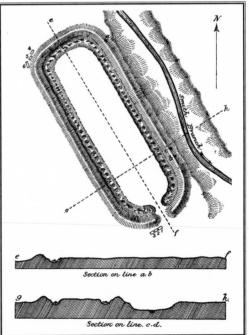

T-35.

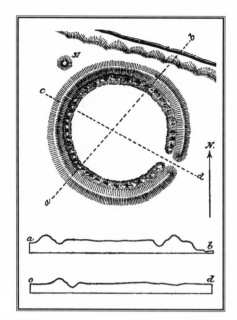

T-36.

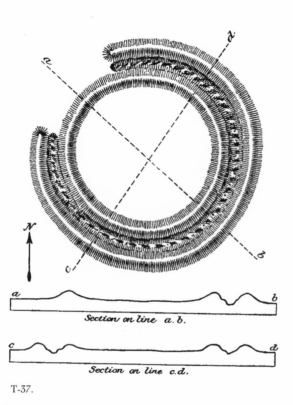

Section on line a.b.

Section on line c.d.

T-37.

T-36.
ENCLOSURE I, NEAR
CHARLESTON

T-37.
ENCLOSURE K, NEAR
CHARLESTON

This figure is intriguing because it is double-circled and the interior circle completely closed.

S-38.
ANCIENT WORK, BOURBON
COUNTY, KENTUCKY

S-38.

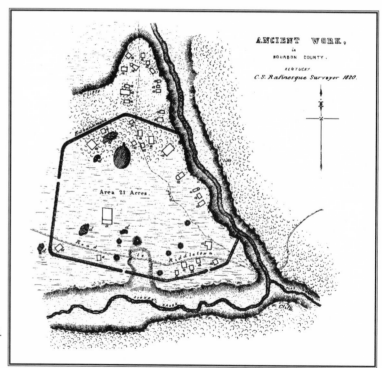

S-39.

ANCIENT WORKS ON BRUSH
CREEK, KENTUCKY

Note D, the hexagonal enclosure
(50 feet per side), and A, the square
with interior moat. Both are unusual
among earthworks.

S-40.

ANCIENT WORKS NEAR WIN-
CHESTER, RANDOLPH COUN-
TY, INDIANA

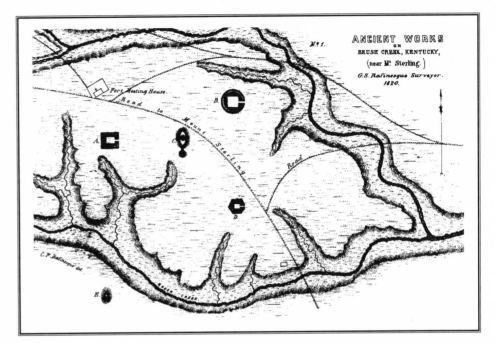

S-39.

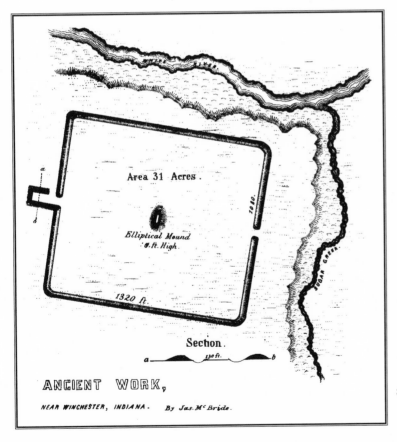

S-40.

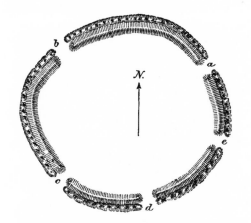

T-41.

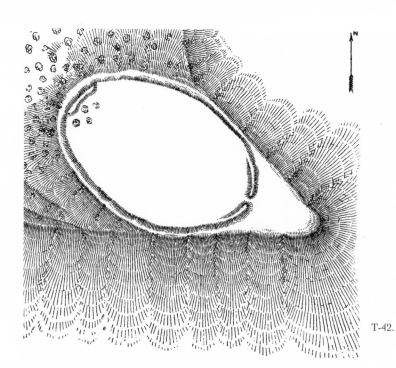

T-42.

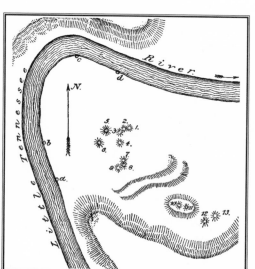

T-43.

T-44.

T-41.
RIFLE RIVER FORT NO. 2,
OGEMAW COUNTY,
MICHIGAN

Note the unusual exterior moat.

T-42.
OLD FORT NEAR ELLINGTON,
CHAUTAUQUA COUNTY,
NEW YORK

T-43.
ENCLOSURE NEAR PITTS-
FIELD, WARREN COUNTY,
PENNSYLVANIA

The enclosure is roughly 320 feet in
diameter. Note the exterior moat.
Thomas remarked on this enclosure's
similarity to the many earthworks in
western New York.

T-44.
MOUNDS ON JOHN
JACKSON'S FARM, LOUDON
COUNTY, TENNESSEE

Most were excavated. Four skeletons
were found in each of mounds No. 6
and No. 11; the burial in No. 3
included a steatite pipe.

T-45.
LENOIR MOUNDS, LOUDON
COUNTY, TENNESSEE

T-46.
SECTION OF MOUND NO. 16
WITH VAULT, DUNLEITH,
ILLINOIS

A 13-foot-long, 7-foot-wide vault
built of stone and logs was found in
this 10-foot mound. It contained 11
skeletons accompanied by a seashell
drinking cup and broken pottery.

T-47.
ANCIENT WORKS ON
BOULWARE'S PLACE,
CLARKE COUNTY, MISSOURI

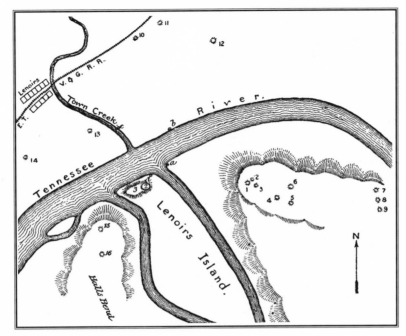

T-45.

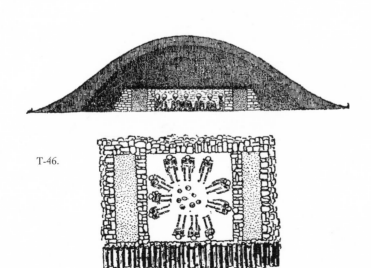

T-46.

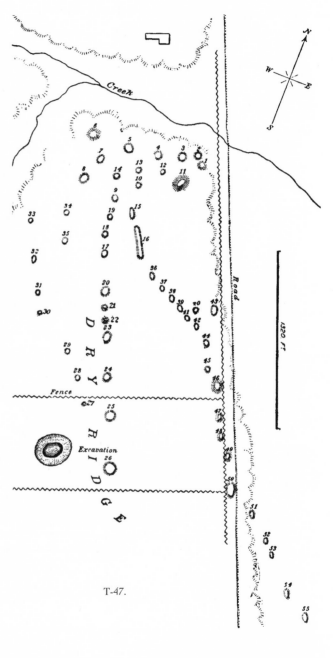

T-47.

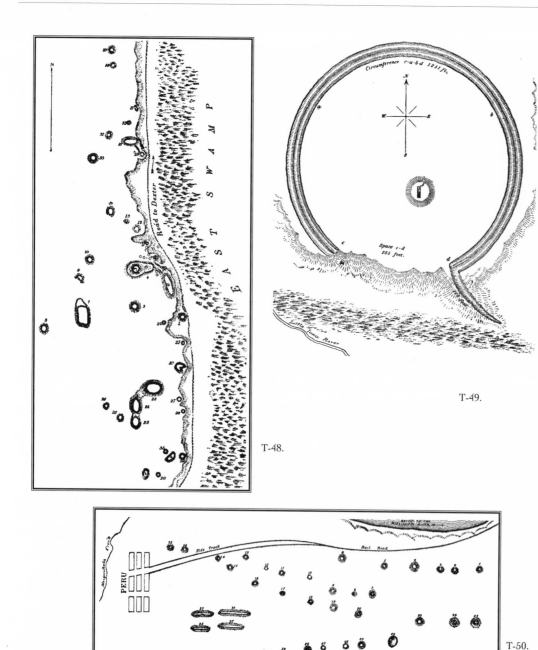

T-48.

T-49.

T-50.

T-51.

T-48.
RICH WOODS MOUNDS,
STODDARD COUNTY,
MISSOURI

T-49.
ENCLOSURE ON HAYS'S
FARM, ALLAMAKEE COUNTY,
IOWA

The circle consisted of three parallel
ditches and two intermediate earthen
walls.

T-50.
GROUP NEAR PERU,
DUBUQUE COUNTY, IOWA

T-51.
DIAGRAM OF INDIAN
BATTLEGROUND, WAPELLO
COUNTY, IOWA

T-52.
ANCIENT WORKS NEAR NEW
ALBIN, ALLAMAKEE COUNTY,
IOWA

Circle A was about 250 feet in diameter. South of the circle there were
originally more than 100 mounds.
These and the ground between were
used as burial places. The prominent
feature *c* in the center is a sand butte
100 to 150 feet high with small
mounds on its crest.

T-53.
VILAS AND FLUCKE GROUPS,
CRAWFORD COUNTY,
WISCONSIN

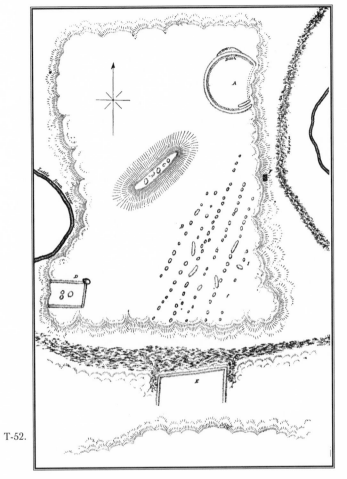

T-52.

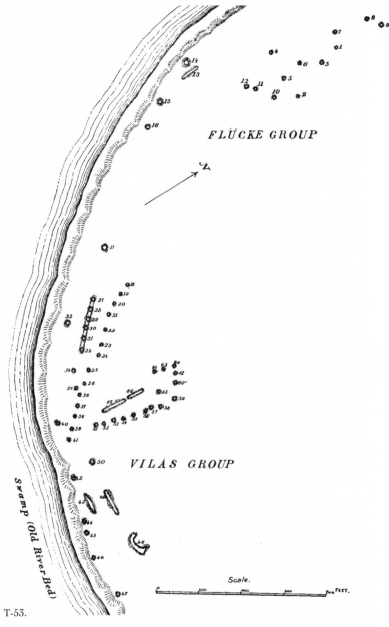

T-53.

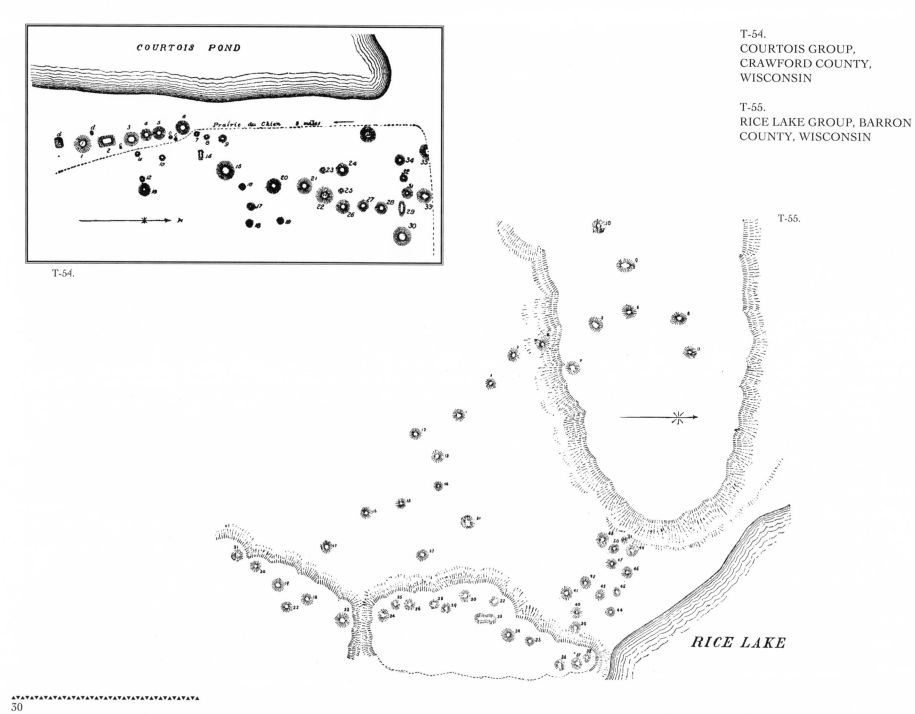

T-54.
COURTOIS GROUP,
CRAWFORD COUNTY,
WISCONSIN

T-55.
RICE LAKE GROUP, BARRON
COUNTY, WISCONSIN

EFFIGY MOUNDS OF NATIVE AMERICA

As the Ohio Hopewell mysteriously were disappearing around AD 500, there arose in the Wisconsin and Iowa areas a tradition of low earthen platforms in the shapes of animals, birds, and even human beings. Whether or not directly descended from such Ohio effigy mounds as the Serpent, this Effigy Mound tradition continued throughout the next era of Native America into the modern period. (Some evidence from the early Lakotah indicates that the effigies may sometimes have been treaty mounds in totemic shapes within which the casualties of wars were interred.)

S-56.
EFFIGY MOUNDS, DADE COUNTY, WISCONSIN

Situated along the Great Indian Trail, the site covers about 1 and 1/2 miles. The animals may be buffalo; the oblongs emphasize a typical alignment along ridges.

S-56.

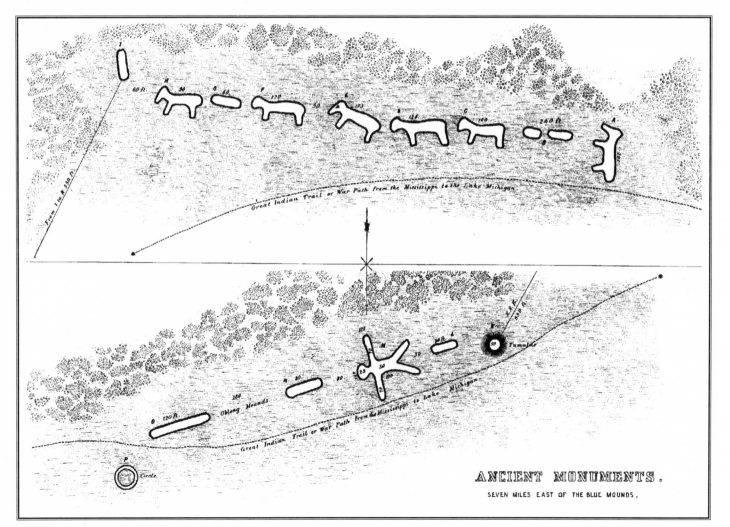

ANCIENT MONUMENTS.
SEVEN MILES EAST OF THE BLUE MOUNDS,

S-57.
EFFIGIES, DADE COUNTY,
WISCONSIN

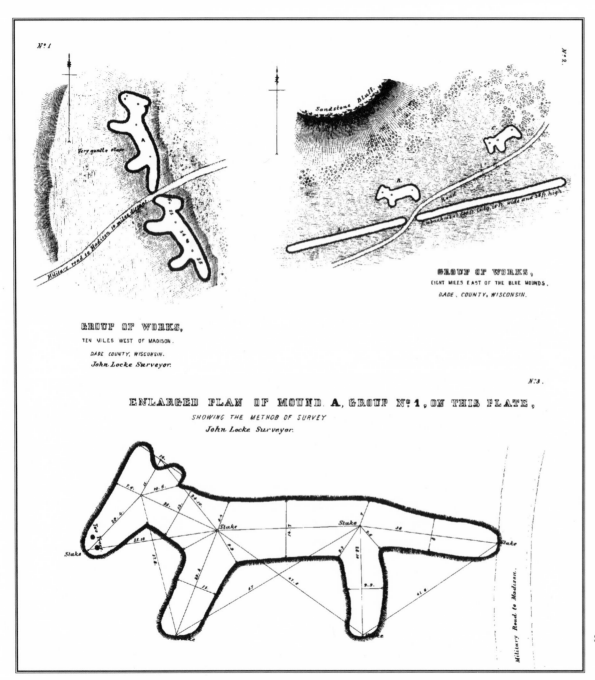

GROUP OF WORKS,
TEN MILES WEST OF MADISON.
DADE COUNTY, WISCONSIN.
John Locke Surveyor.

GROUP OF WORKS,
EIGHT MILES EAST OF THE BLUE MOUNDS.
DADE, COUNTY, WISCONSIN.

ENLARGED PLAN OF MOUND A, GROUP N° 1, ON THIS PLATE,
SHOWING THE METHOD OF SURVEY
John Locke Surveyor.

S-57.

S-58.
EFFIGIES, DADE AND
RICHLAND COUNTIES,
WISCONSIN

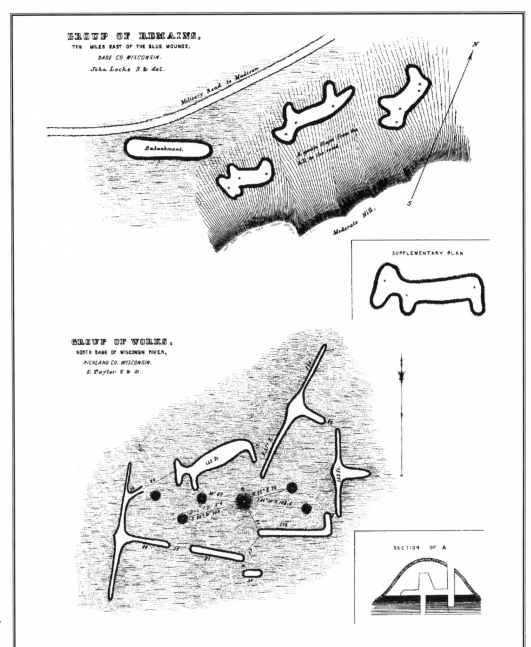

S-58.

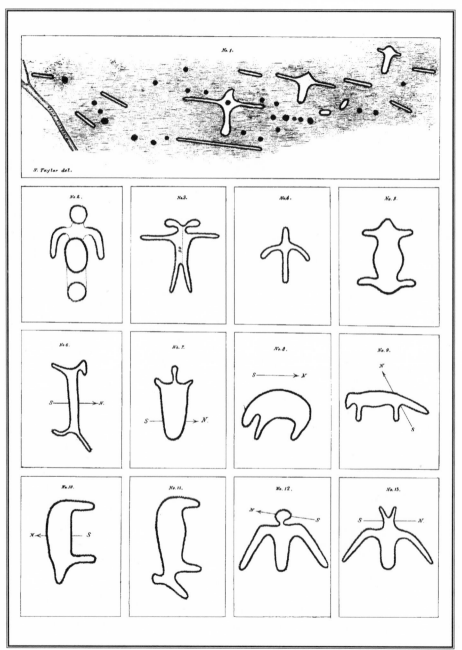

S-59.

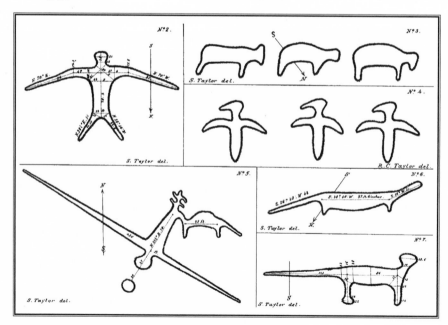

S-59.
EFFIGIES, GRANT COUNTY,
WISCONSIN

S-60.
EFFIGIES, WISCONSIN

S-60.

T-61.
SOUTHWESTERN CRAWFORD
COUNTY, WISCONSIN

There were 37 groups of earthworks
within the junction of the Wisconsin
and Mississippi Rivers. Mound sites
were also frequent across the river in
Iowa.

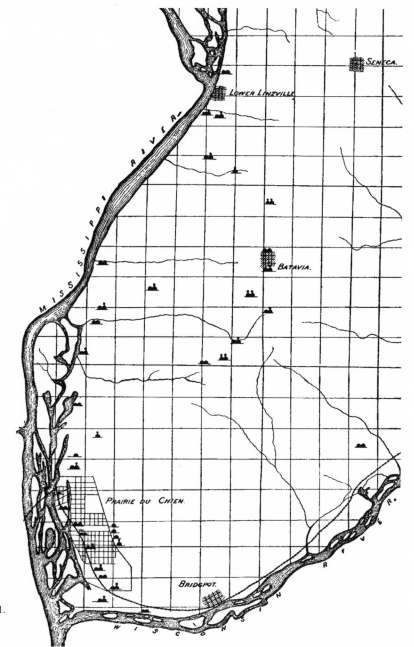

T-61.

T-62.

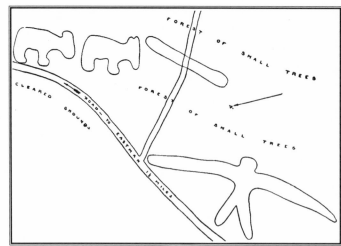

T-62.
EFFIGIES, CRAWFORD
COUNTY, WISCONSIN

Note the encroachment of roads on
the site.

T-63.
MOUND GROUP, HAZEN COR-
NERS, CRAWFORD COUNTY,
WISCONSIN

The damage caused by roads is clear.

T-64.
BIRD EFFIGIES, HAZEN
CORNERS

The Effigy Mound peoples continued the Hopewell reverence of the
bird.

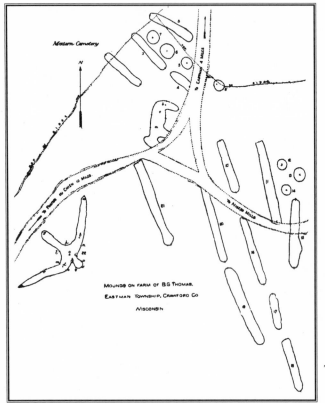

T-63.

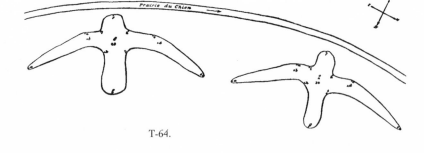

T-64.

T-65.
GROUP OF BIRD EFFIGIES,
HAZEN CORNERS

T-66.
EFFIGY MOUNDS NEAR
CASSVILLE, GRANT COUNTY,
WISCONSIN

T-67.
MOUND GROUP NEAR
WYALUSING, GRANT
COUNTY, WISCONSIN

T-65.

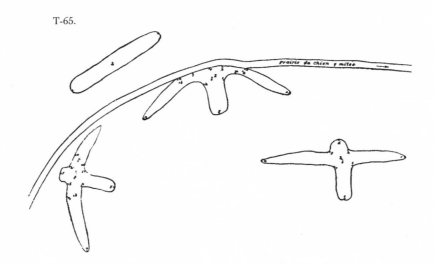

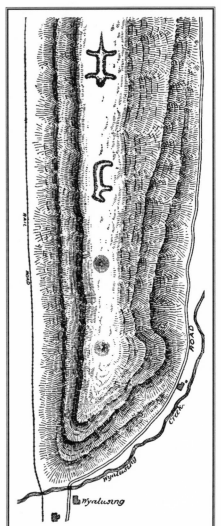

T-67.

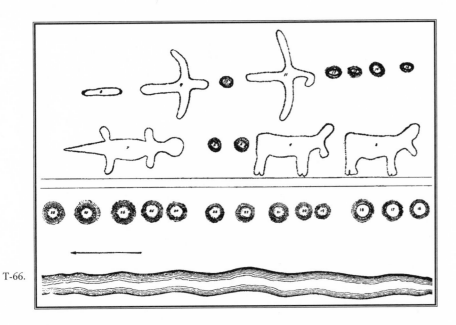

T-66.

68.

68.
MARCHING BEAR GROUP, CLAYTON COUNTY, IOWA

The second largest group of effigy mounds remaining in the United States, it follows a ridgetop above the Mississippi River. It is part of Effigy Mounds National Monument. Allan Zarling, Photographer.

T-69.
ENCLOSURES AND MOUNDS, PIPESTONE COUNTY, MINNESOTA

This far distant region was the source of the red stone (catlinite) preferred by Native Americans for carving pipes. These earthworks near the sacred pipestone quarry and pipes found in Ohio reveal the site's long history. It is now a National Monument.

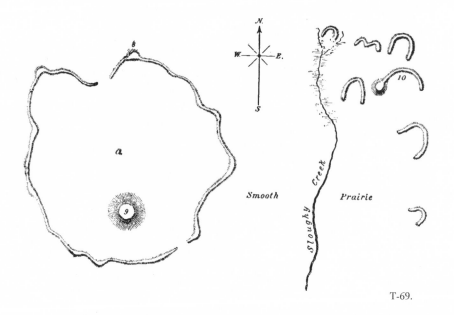

T-69.

▲▼

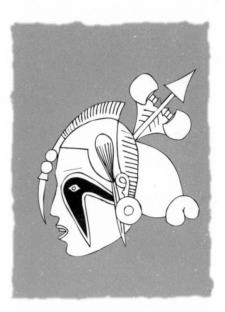

THE MISSISSIPPI PERIOD IS RIGHTFULLY viewed the Classic stage of eastern Native American civilizations. Across the drainage of the vast Mississippi River system and throughout the Southeast, over several centuries, the peoples neighboring the Ohio-era Hopewell transformed their villages into towns and cities. They continued the ancient practice of mound burial for important personages, but dramatically changed other earthworking traditions.

Illustration: WARRIOR HEAD—Detail, inscribed marine shell cup, AD 1100 - 1250, Spiro site, Le Flore County, Oklahoma Dimensions and location unknown

The forked or weeping eye design on the face occurs frequently and may derive from the patterning on the face of the peregrine falcon. The hairbun is restored in accordance with other heads on the same cup.

The hallmark of Mississippi-era earthworking was flattopped pyramidal temple mounds around a central plaza, suggestive of both complex social and religious organization and reminiscent of Meso-American architectural forms. Trade contacts with the Maya best explain the pyramid tradition which first appeared by AD 400 to 500 along the Florida Gulf Coast at Crystal River and Fort Walton, and in

Continued on Page 41

70.

DISTRIBUTION OF LATE MISSISSIPPIAN CIVILIZATIONS (AD 1200 - 1400)

The map also identifies neighboring non-Mississippian (i.e., non- pyramid building) peoples of the era. These include the previously mentioned effigy-mound building peoples, the Oneota.

There were numerous reports from the earliest French explorers ascending the St. Lawrence of Algonquins and Hurons in towns and cities surrounded by log palisades.

The Siouan peoples of the middle Atlantic originally shared the coastal cultural traditions of the Irene and Timucua peoples of the southern Atlantic coast. Shortly after their first encounters with Europeans, the Sioux began migrating to the plains, thus invading the Oneota region. There they adapted their lifeway to the buffalo and the horse and became the modern iconic image of the war-bonneted Native American.

The Iroquois of the St. Lawrence River valley were actually of Mississippian Caddo stock, who by AD 1300 migrated up the Ohio to the far northeast. In the course of their migration they abandoned traditional Mississippian culture and developed a remarkable one of their own which included long-house architecture and a republican form of government that influenced the framers of the United States Constitution.

The Kiowa of the southern plains most likely served as a link between the Anasazi cultures of the Desert Southwest and the Mississippian Caddo.

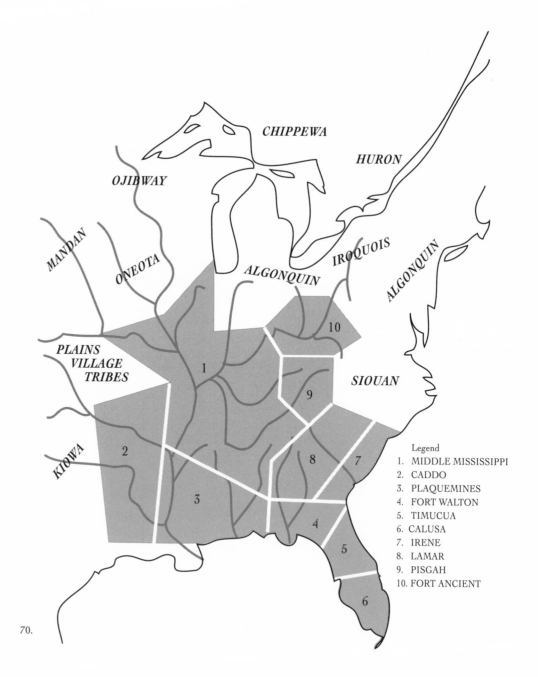

Legend
1. MIDDLE MISSISSIPPI
2. CADDO
3. PLAQUEMINES
4. FORT WALTON
5. TIMUCUA
6. CALUSA
7. IRENE
8. LAMAR
9. PISGAH
10. FORT ANCIENT

70.

lower Louisiana at Troyville and Marksville. To this design were added embanked enclosures frequently topped with palisaded log walls for defense.

Spreading inland and upriver from those first contacts, a multitude of Mississippian urban centers, dependent on river locations for their maize agriculture and on forests for hunting, flourished by AD 1200 over a vast area of nearly a half-million square miles from Oklahoma and eastern Texas to North Carolina, and from Wisconsin to the very tip of the Florida peninsula.

The greatest of the cities was Cahokia in Illinois, located across the river from present-day St. Louis near the town of Collinsville. The population of this ancient metropolis is estimated to have been 40,000 at its peak circa AD 1400. Smaller cities such as Moundville in Alabama, though not equal in size, were most definitely important cultural centers of Mississippian civilization.

It was only at the fringes of this vast civilization, perhaps already in decline, that early European explorers came into contact with the Mississippians.

By the mid sixteenth century, de Soto and his troops marched through the southeastern heartland, both providing the earliest written records of these Native Americans and leaving behind new diseases that accelerated the collapse of their world.

Though the many cities and towns of the Mississippian peoples have passed away, elements of their culture survive among tribes such as the Cherokee, Creek, and Choctaw. Now, after 500 years, it is indeed time to pay homage to this truly ancient heritage of Native Americans.

71.

MARKSVILLE SITE,
AVOYELLES PARISH,
LOUISIANA (200 BC - AD 600)

Located on Old River, a former channel of the Mississippi River, this is one of the earliest occurrences of the pyramid. Many burial mounds and Ohioan circular enclosures in the vicinity reflect the site's earlier heritage. It is now a State Commemorative Area.

71.

T-72.

TROYVILLE MOUNDS, CATA-HOULA PARISH, LOUISIANA

The wall was about 1 mile long and 7 to 8 feet high, enclosing 100 acres. The large central mound was said to have been nearly 75 feet high with a sharp summit, but in Thomas's time stood only at 45 feet, having been used during the Civil War as a location for rifle pits.

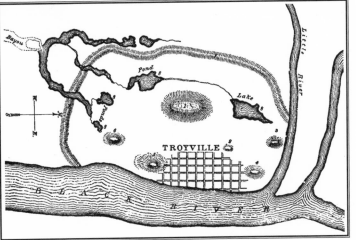

T-72.

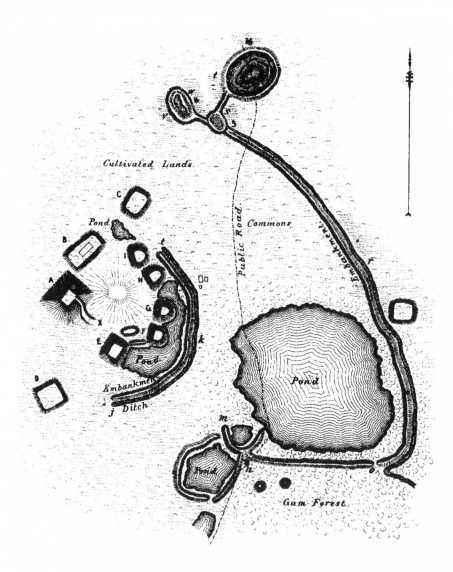

Cultivated Lands.

C

Pond

B

A

Public Road.

Commons

Embankment

t

H

G

f

E

k

Pond

Embankment

j Ditch

D

Pond

m

Wood

n

Gum Forest

ANCIENT WORKS,

PRAIRIE JEFFERSON, MOORHOUSE PARISH,

LOUISIANA.

C.G. Forshey Surveyor.

S-74.

T-73. VIEW OF MOUND NO. 6,
TROYVILLE

S-74.
ANCIENT WORKS,
MOORHOUSE PARISH,
LOUISIANA

The embankments were apparently
designed for flood control and water
supply. Mound A was 48 feet high.

T-73.

S-75.
ANCIENT MONUMENTS, MADISON PARISH, LOUISIANA

The largest pyramid was 30 feet high, the elevated way 3 feet high. The earlier Maya of Yucatan also constructed elevated roadways. This site was under cultivation in Squier's time.

76.
EMERALD SITE, ADAMS COUNTY, MISSISSIPPI

Overlooking the Natchez Trace, the site was still occupied by the Natchez when the French arrived in the 1600s. A huge pentagonal platform with two pyramids and other conical mounds atop, it was the ceremonial seat of their god-king, the Great Sun, upon whom the general Mississippian socio-religious system apparently was based. The view is from one pyramid to the other.

S-75.

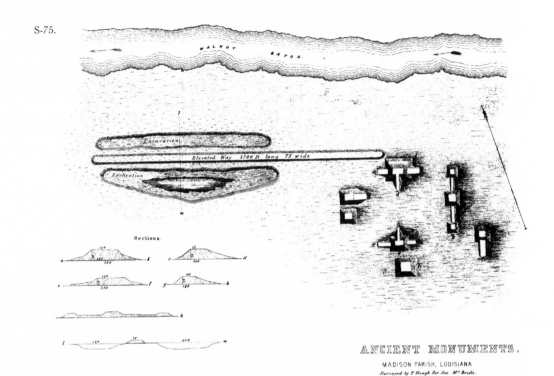

ANCIENT MONUMENTS.
MADISON PARISH, LOUISIANA
Surveyed by T. Hough for Jas. M. Bride.

76.

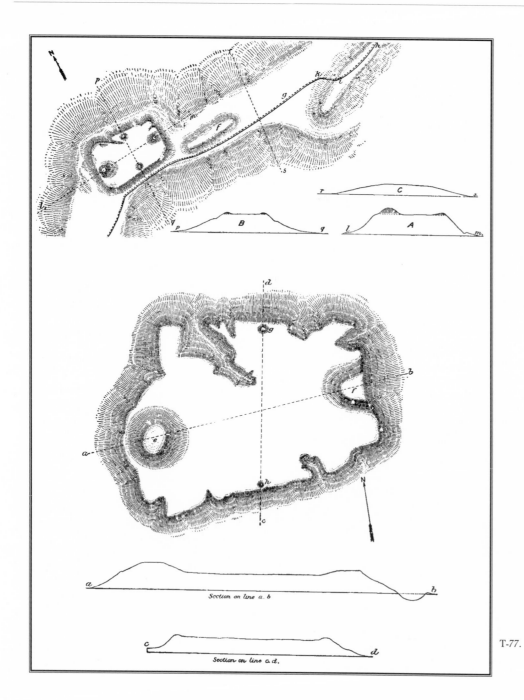

T-77.

T-77.
SELSERTOWN GROUP,
ADAMS COUNTY, MISSISSIPPI

The lower platform was already
much eroded. Mound e at the western end was 31 feet high.

T-78.
AVONDALE MOUNDS, WASHINGTON COUNTY, MISSISSIPPI

"The largest [mound], which is used as a graveyard by the whites, is 30 feet high, flat on top, and oval in form, nearly 200 feet long and about 175 broad... The second is 15 feet high and is covered with graves of colored people." — *Thomas*.

79.
WINTERVILLE SITE, WASHINGTON COUNTY, MISSISSIPPI

This large double-ramped pyramid was surrounded by some 24 residence and temple mounds of varying heights. The site has been identified with the city of Quizquiz in de Soto's time. Only this and a smaller pyramid now exist in a park with the Winterville Mounds Museum.

T-78.

79.

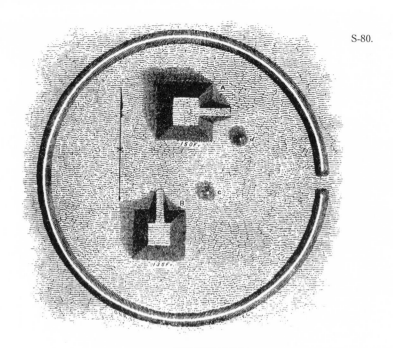

S-80.

WORKS IN BOLIVAR COUNTY, MISSISSIPPI

This Hopewell-like circle was 2,300 feet in circumference and 4 feet high. Pyramid A was 20 feet high and Pyramid B 15 feet. Both are aligned with the cardinal points.

T-81.
CARSON MOUNDS, COAHOMA COUNTY, MISSISSIPPI

Located on an old channel of the Mississippi River, the site contained some very unique earthworks. The double Mound *b* (left center) was quite complex: "There are at the bottom indications of an oval platform, probably 10 feet high, with a length of 240 feet at the base. On this, two truncated cones, which occupy the entire length, but not the entire width of the platform, rise jointly for 18 feet, and above the union rise separately 8 feet higher. The entire height of the mound from the natural surface of the land is therefore 36 feet. The cones are level on top, the one being 42 feet in diameter at this point, and the other 48." — *Thomas.* Mound *∂* was then the finest of the group, "roughly pentangular and very symmetrical, level on the top, 25 feet high (including the platform), 310 feet in diameter at the base, and 210 feet across the top."

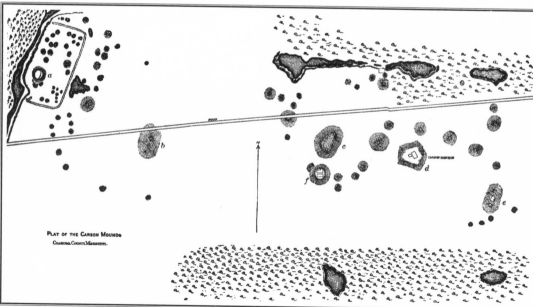

PLAT OF THE CARSON MOUNDS
Coahoma County, Mississippi.

T-81.

T-82.
MOUND GROUP,
UNION COUNTY, MISSISSIPPI

"Before the soil had been cultivated, an embankment could be traced around the 12 central mounds, which was about 2 feet high and 10 feet across at the base, with a ditch on the outside entirely around." — *Thomas*. Testifying to the continuity of Mississippian civilization up to historic times, in Mound 3 were found an iron knife and a thin silver plate stamped with the Spanish coat of arms, possibly souvenirs of de Soto's passing.

T-83.
OLD TOWN WORKS, PHILLIPS
COUNTY, ARKANSAS

The small light circles indicate house sites.

T-82.

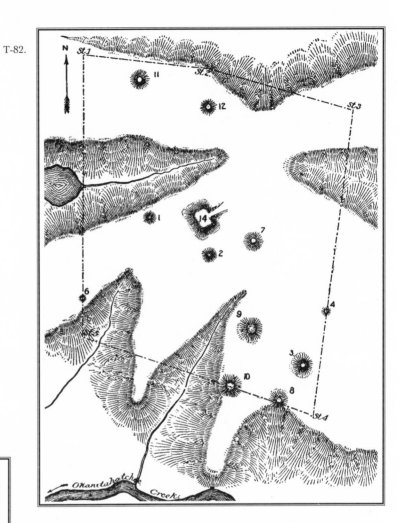

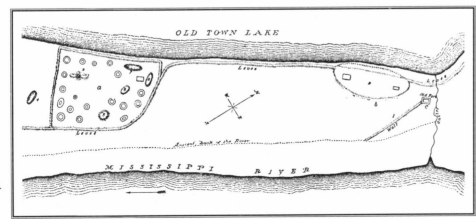

T-83.

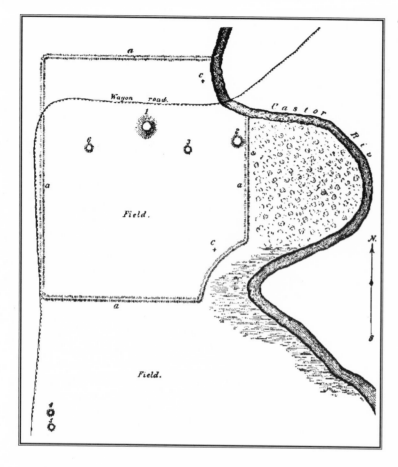

T-84.

T-84.
PETER BESS SETTLEMENT,
BOLLINGER COUNTY,
MISSOURI

T-85.
LAKEVILLE SETTLEMENT,
STODDARD COUNTY,
MISSOURI

Note the house sites.

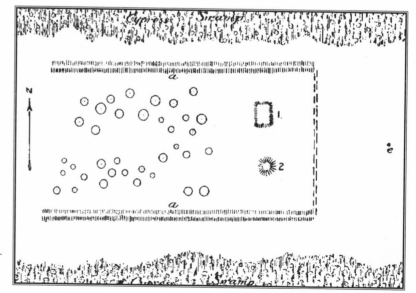

T-85.

86.
TOWASEGHY SITE,
MISSISSIPPI COUNTY,
MISSOURI

Of three pyramids, two are on state land. The third serves as a foundation for a barn.

T-87.
POWER'S FORT, BUTLER COUNTY, MISSOURI

There was an outside ditch along the entire length of the walls. Mound No. 1 was 20 feet high, but it had already been cultivated for fifty years by Thomas's time.

86.

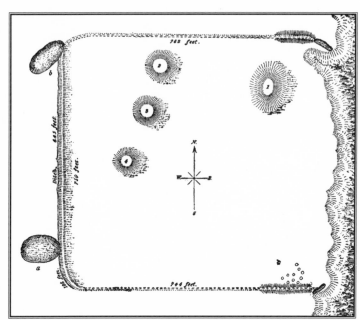

T-87.

88.
PINSON MOUNDS,
MADISON COUNTY,
TENNESSEE

This 72-foot pyramid, known as
Mound 9 or Sauls Mound, is the
second highest earthwork of ancient
America. It has corners roughly
aligned with the cardinal points
and may have had a ramp on the
northeast side. Photo courtesy
Pinson Mounds State Archaeological Area.

88.

T-89.
O'BYAM'S FORT,
HICKMAN COUNTY,
KENTUCKY

On a 50-foot bluff, this work
retained traces of numerous house
rings shown here as small circles.

90.
WICKLIFFE MOUNDS,
BALLARD COUNTY,
KENTUCKY

Located near the confluence of the
Mississippi and Ohio Rivers, this
site's earthworks have suffered much
damage. Photo courtesy Wickliffe
Mounds Research Center.

T-89.

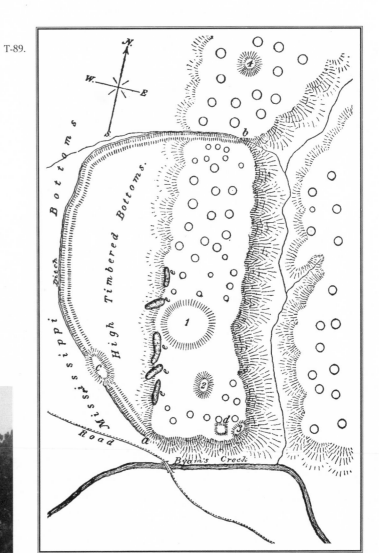

90.

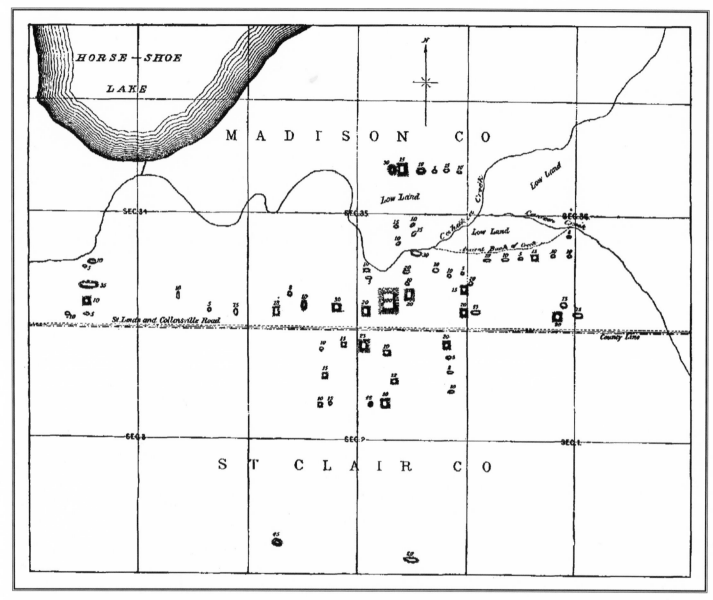

T-91.

Cahokia was the largest known Mississippian center. The map indicates the great number of mounds at the site, but not the vast turreted palisade of logs which encircled the principal area. Nor does it indicate the magnitude of the earthworks. The central complex pyramid, Monk's Mound, almost 100 feet high, is the largest earthwork by volume in the world. Other large centers also existed across the river on the site of present-day St. Louis and just upriver in Illinois.

Most of the smaller mounds, of which there were over 60 others in the near vicinity, are now gone. A freeway skirts the site and a road runs across it. The central portion, a State Historic Site with an exceptional interpretive center, has been designated a United Nations World Heritage Site (which list includes the pyramids of Egypt, the city of Rome, the Great Wall of China, and the Taj Mahal in India, among other important sites).

92.
COMMUNITY LIFE AT CAHOKIA

Located at the Interpretive Center, this mural by Michael Hampshire depicts daily activities, including house construction and crafts. Cahokia's ruler, the Great Sun, is carried in procession across the central plaza from his residence on Monk's Mound.

93.
WOODHENGE

This painting by L. K. Townsend, also at the Interpretive Center, portrays the erection of the Woodhenge sun calendar. Researchers have found post-molds of large circles of poles for determining solstice and equinox.

92.

93.

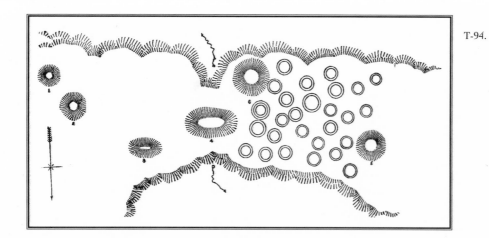

T-94.

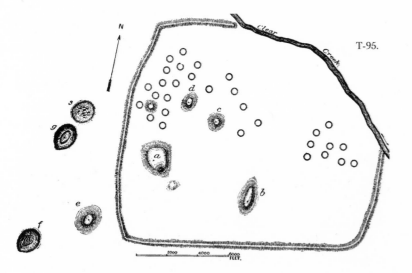

T-95.

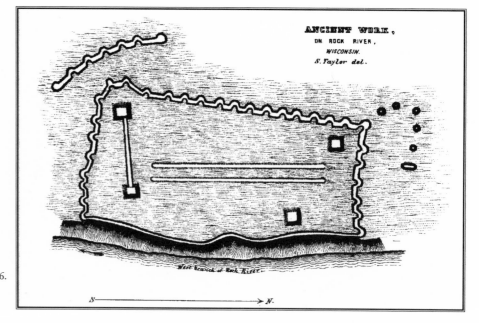

S-96.

T-94.
WELCH GROUP,
BROWN COUNTY, ILLINOIS

In Thomas's time the site was cultivated in wheat.

T-95.
WORKS ON LINN'S PLACE,
UNION COUNTY, ILLINOIS

S-96.
ANCIENT WORKS ON ROCK
RIVER, JEFFERSON COUNTY,
WISCONSIN

An outpost of the Mississippian culture was established even as far north as what is now Madison, Wisconsin. The site is now in Aztalan State Park.

T-97.
ANGEL MOUNDS, EVANS-
VILLE, VANDERBURGH
COUNTY, INDIANA

The Mississippian influence spread
up the Ohio River. Angel Mounds is
a State Historic Site.

S-98. ANCIENT WORKS,
MARIETTA, WASHINGTON
COUNTY, OHIO

At this venerable Ohioan site the
new Mississippians also raised their
pyramids. It was the farthest point of
their northeastward expansion. Note
the Great Mound in the distance, by
then already ancient.

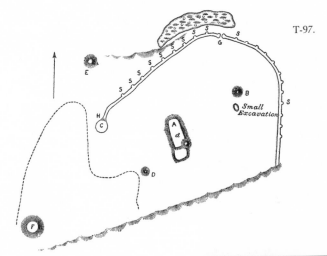

T-97.

S-98.

99.

99.
CRYSTAL RIVER SITE, CITRUS COUNTY, FLORIDA (200 BC - AD 1400)

The site was transitional from the Ohio to the Mississippi eras. Besides this unusual rectangular pyramid and another square one, there were also two much deteriorated stelae, the only examples of that Meso-American practice in North America. Other mounds found here are heaps of seashell refuse, common in coastal areas. (Heaps of freshwater mussel shells also occur in the Tennessee River valley.) The works are presently a State Archaeological Site and National Historic Landmark.

100. SAFETY HARBOR SITE, PINELLAS COUNTY, FLORIDA

The area around Tampa Bay was well populated and was the site of several Mississippian towns with their attendant temple and burial mounds. Safety Harbor, a later site of the Calusa on the north shore of the bay, could well have been the landing place for de Soto's expedition. The site is now a National Historic Landmark in Phillippe Park. Photograph courtesy Pinellas County Park Department.

100.

101.
LAKE JACKSON MOUNDS,
LEON COUNTY, FLORIDA

This large pyramid and smaller
surrounding mounds composed the
principal complex among those
around the lakeshore. The site was
very possibly the city of Appalachee
which was conquered by de Soto
early in his expedition. Similar complexes also existed on the local Lakes
Miccosukee and Lafayette. Lake
Jackson Mounds is now a State
Archaeological Site.

101.

102.

102.
VIEW OF MOUND C,
ETOWAH SITE,
BARTOW COUNTY, GEORGIA

The view is from atop the largest
pyramid on Mound C which was the
source of several remarkable artifacts. The site boasted a plaza paved
with special red clay. The larger
mounds are preserved in the Etowah
Indian Mounds State Historic Site.

103.
OCMULGEE SITE, BIBB COUNTY, GEORGIA

This site was apparently an early intrusive settlement of Middle Mississippians on the Macon Plateau. It includes this reconstructed earthlodge, of which there were originally several. The entrance at left leads through a tunnel to a large log-framed circular chamber containing a raised clay platform shaped like a bird and bench around the perimeter with some 50 seats. Its ground plan and probable ceremonial function are reminiscent of the kivas of the Southwest. A railroad now crosses the site and has destroyed part of a mound. Photograph courtesy Ocmulgee National Monument.

103.

104.
ROCK EAGLE, PUTNAM COUNTY, GEORGIA

This unusual effigy mound of heaped rocks is a striking continuation of the ancient bird motif which pervaded Mississippian culture. Photograph courtesy Rock Eagle 4-H Center.

104.

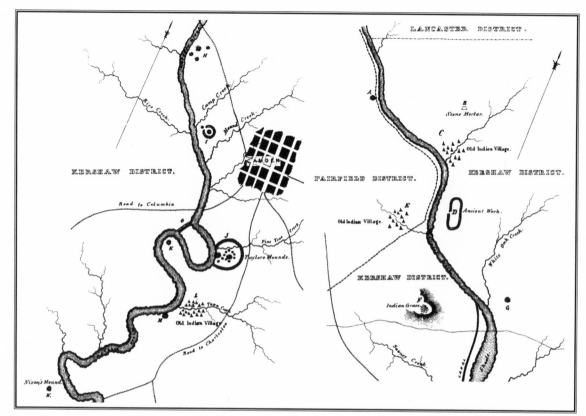

S-105

106.
PALISADE AT TOWN CREEK
MOUND, MONTGOMERY
COUNTY, NORTH CAROLINA

A log palisade of the type that surrounded most Mississippian towns
has been reconstructed around a
temple pyramid and plaza. Shown
here is a corner turret and gate.
Photograph courtesy Town Creek
Indian Mound State Historic Site.

106.

T-107.
TIMBERLAKE'S MAP OF
OVERHILL CHEROKEE
TOWNS

The Cherokee, descendants of the
Pisgah peoples, continued some Mississippian traditions well into the
eighteenth century in eastern Tennessee and western North Carolina.

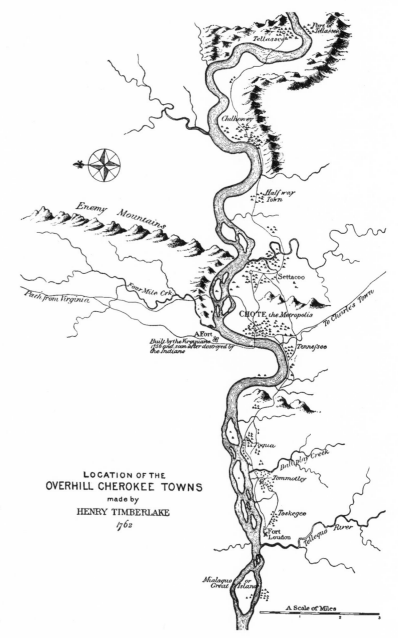

T-107.

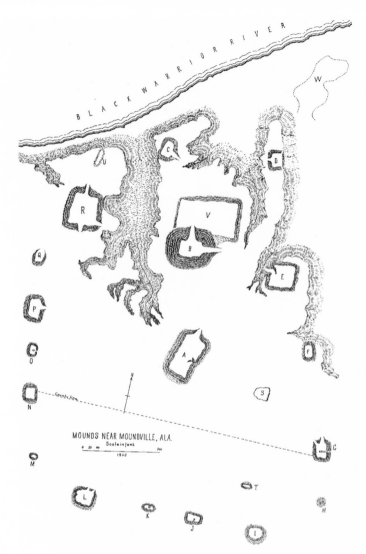

108.

MOUNDS NEAR MOUNDVILLE, ALA.
Scale in feet
1905

108.
MOUNDVILLE SITE, HALE COUNTY, ALABAMA

This site on the Black Warrior River was one of the major Mississippian centers. Mound B with double ramps and raised plaza V was the temple pyramid. The encircling smaller platforms were residence mounds. The map is from Moore, 1905 (see Reading List). Most of the mounds are well preserved as Moundville Archaeological Park, which is a National Historic Landmark.

109.
ON THE PLAZA AT MOUNDVILLE

This view is of Mound A from Mound B.

109.

WESTERN MISSISSIPPI — THE CADDO

The Mississippian culture extended as far west as Spiro in northeastern Oklahoma which flourished from AD 900 to 1250. Affected by the deteriorating climate of the Southwest, which also impacted the neighboring Plains Village peoples, the Spiro area populations migrated. Many were absorbed by Caddo peoples in the Arkansas and east Texas areas. Others became the Iroquois.

The Mississippian Caddo hold the distinction of being the ones who finally turned back de Soto's troops. Seriously demoralized by the rigors of their trek all the way from Tampa, Florida via Tennessee, the Spaniards were then driven by the Plaquemines peoples down the Mississippi River to the Gulf of Mexico.

110.
CRAIG MOUND, SPIRO SITE, LE FLORE COUNTY, OKLAHOMA

Before being protected, the large Craig Mound was mined for souvenirs. Thus many artifacts disappeared forever. The documented finds, however, are some of the most remarkable of all pre-Columbian Native American works of art. The site is now Spiro Mounds Archeological State Park.

110.

111.

111.
CADDOAN MOUNDS, CHEROKEE COUNTY, TEXAS

This large temple mound, which was also used for burials, is one of three mounds at the site. Many other mounds occur in the vicinity on private land. Photograph courtesy Caddoan Mounds State Historic Park.

T-112. MENARD MOUNDS, ARKANSAS COUNTY, ARKANSAS

Mound *a*, 50 feet high, was very steep and was flanked by two platforms, one 20 and the other 7 feet high. The smaller, much lower mounds were house sites.

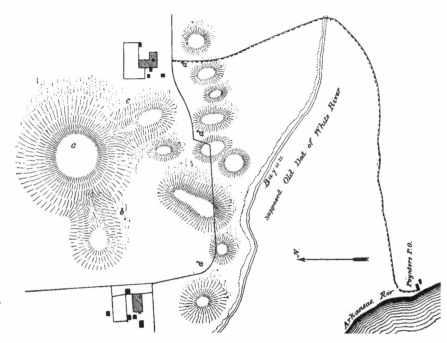

T-112.

T-113.
TAYLOR SHANTY GROUP, POINSETT COUNTY, ARKANSAS

At left, Mound No. 14 at 6 feet was the highest. Mound No. 1, a large platform of roughly the same height, was much eroded by the overflow of the St. Francis River by Thomas's time.

T-114.
MOUNDS AT TYRONZA STATION, POINSETT COUNTY, ARKANSAS

Note the intrusion of a railroad siding and gravel pit on the site. Mound No. 1 was 12 feet high and most of the rest 5 to 9 feet. Several of the smaller were house mounds.

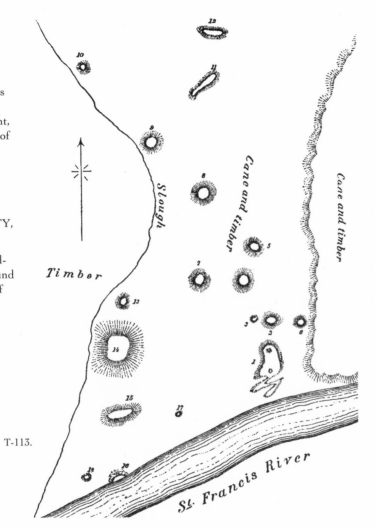

T-113.

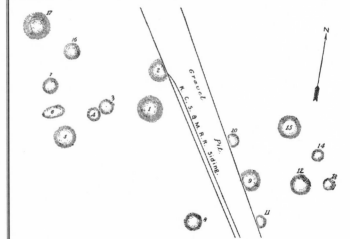

T-114.

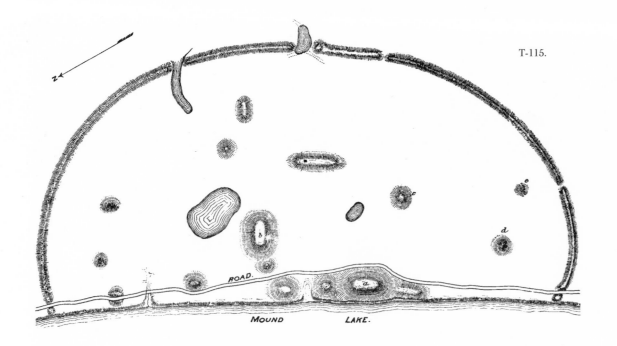

T-115.

T-116.

T-117.

T-115.
KNAPP MOUNDS, PULASKI COUNTY, ARKANSAS

Located on Mound Lake, a crescent-shaped bayou, the Knapp Mounds lie 16 miles southeast of Little Rock. The earthworks have been studied to determine possible astronomical alignment. The site is protected in the Toltec Mounds Archeological State Park.

T-116. KNAPP MOUNDS, PULASKI COUNTY, ARKANSAS

Because the works are on a field 2 to 6 feet above the average water level, the surrounding earthen wall is about 6 feet high. Mound *a* is the highest at 48 feet. Mound *b* is 38 feet.

T-117.
DE SOTO MOUND, JEFFERSON COUNTY, ARKANSAS

The de Soto Mound is 60 feet high at the west end. A large pond behind was formed during its construction. The name reflects the local traditional belief that the explorer camped here.

T-118.
MOUND NEAR ARKANSAS
CITY, DESHA COUNTY,
ARKANSAS

T-119.
BRADLEY MOUNDS,
CRITTENDEN COUNTY,
ARKANSAS

Some 70 intact pottery vessels were
obtained during excavations.

T-120.
HUGHES MOUND,
SALINE COUNTY, ARKANSAS

T-118.

T-119.

T-120.

T-121.

T-121.
TAYLOR MOUNDS,
DREW COUNTY, ARKANSAS

One large flattopped and terraced mound, 30 feet high, is not shown in the illustration. The mounds and house sites "had been opened and rifled of their treasures previous to the visit of the Bureau agent."
—*Thomas*.

EPILOGUE

The earthworks of ancient America—and the Native Americans who raised them—must not be forgotten!

The Ohio era ceremonial works are or, more appropriately and regrettably, were among the world's most magnificent achievements in earthworking art, rivaling even the wonders of the Old World. Unique masterpieces of another kind of earthworking are the Serpent in Ohio and the effigy mounds of Iowa and Wisconsin. The pyramidal temple mounds of the Mississippi era, which exceeded the famous Mayan and Aztec pyramids in number and often in magnitude, took earthworking to a truly monumental level.

All Native American earthworks that have survived should be stringently protected, and the communities where they are found should take pride in their ancient monuments. The major sites of Arkansas, Ohio, and Mississippi are deserving of official designation as National Monuments.

Poverty Point in Louisiana is at last in the process of becoming a National Monument—a fitting commemoration for 1992. However, of Ohio era earthworks, only the Mound City Group, a single embanked area of mortuary mounds near Chillicothe, Ohio, is a National Monument. Other well-honored sites are Effigy Mounds National Monument in Iowa and Pipestone National Mounument in Minnesota. Representing the Mississippian world, there is only one National Monument—Ocmulgee in Georgia.

A more realistic list of National Monuments, one which would truly honor the great history of Native America, would include, at the very minimum, the Serpent, the remnants of the Newark Works, and Fort Ancient in Ohio; Cahokia in Illinois; and Moundville in Alabama. Sites already recognized and protected by various states—Marksville in Louisiana, Emerald in Mississippi, Crystal River in Florida, Etowah in Georgia, Toltec in Arkansas, Spiro in Oklahoma, Angel in Indiana, Aztalan in Wisconsin, and many others—should at least be elevated to the status of National Memorials, National Historic Sites, National Historic Parks, or National Historic Landmarks.

These ancient Native American earthworks, the handiwork of the Arkansas, Ohio, and Mississippi peoples, are national treasures of the United States. We, today's Americans, need only awaken to the legacy of these ancient peoples, and awakening, see these wonders that existed before Columbus, and seeing, remember Native America!

▲▽▲

The following list is by no means exhaustive as many towns and counties have local earthworks which are not acknowledged as historic landmarks or public attractions.

ALABAMA

Indian Mound Museum, South Court St., Florence, AL 35630. 205/760-6427

Moundville Archaeological Park, P.O. Box 66, Moundville, AL 35474. 205/371-2572

ARKANSAS

Parkin Mound Archeological State Park (under development)

Toltec Mounds Archeological State Park, #1 Toltec Mounds Rd., Scott, AR 72142-9502. 501/961-9442

FLORIDA

Crystal River State Archaeological Site, 3400 N. Museum Point, Crystal River, FL 32629. 904/795-3817

Indian Temple Mound Museum, City of Ft. Walton Beach, P.O. Box 4009, Ft. Walton Beach, FL 32549. 904/243-6521

Lake Jackson Mounds State Archaeological Site, 1313 Crowder Rd., off US 27N, Tallahassee, FL 32308. 904/562-0042

Safety Harbor State Archaeological Site, Philippe Park, 2355 Bay Shore Dr., Safety Harbor, FL 34695. 813/726-2700

GEORGIA

Etowah Indian Mounds State Historic Site, 813 Indian Mounds Rd. SW, Cartersville, GA 30120. 404/387-3747

Kolomoki Mounds State Historic Park, Rte. 1 Box 114, Blakely, GA 31723. 912/723-5296

Ocmulgee National Monument, 1207 Emery Hwy., Macon, GA 31201. 912/752-8257

Rock Eagle, 350 Rock Eagle Rd., Eatonton, GA 31024. 404/485-2831

ILLINOIS

Cahokia Mounds State Historic Site, P.O. Box 681, 7850 Collinsville Rd., Collinsville, IL 62234. 618/346-5160

Dickson Mounds Museum, RR1 Box 185, Lewistown, IL 61542. 309/547-3721

Piasa Bird Pictograph, Rt. 100 n. of Alton, IL. 618/465-6676

INDIANA

Angel Mounds State Historic Site, 8215 Pollack Ave., Evansville, IN 47715. 812/853-3956

Mounds State Park, 4306 Mounds Rd., Anderson, IN 46017. 317/642-6627

IOWA

Effigy Mounds National Monument, Rte. 1 Box 25A, Harpers Ferry, IA 52146-9744. 319/873-3491

KENTUCKY

Wickliffe Mounds Research Center, P.O. Box 155, Wickliffe, KY 42087. 502/335-3681

LOUISIANA

Marksville State Commemorative Area, 700 Martin Luther King Dr., Marksville, LA 71351. 318/253-8954 or 853-9546

Poverty State Commemorative Area, P. O. Box 248, Epps, LA 71237. 318/926-5492

MINNESOTA

Grand Mound, Rte. 7, Box 453, International Falls, MN 56649. 218/279-3332

Lake Wagonga Mounds, near Kandiyohi

Pipestone National Monument, P.O. Box 727, Pipestone, MN 56164. 507/825-5464

MISSISSIPPI

Emerald Mound, Mount Locust, Rte. 4 Box 250, Natchez, MS 39120. 601/445-4211

Nanih Waiya Historic Park, Rte. 3 Box 251A, Louisville, MS 39339. 601/773-7988

Winterville Mound Museum, Hwy 1, Rte. 3, Greenville, MS 38703. 601/334-4684

MISSOURI

Van Meter State Park, Rte. 1 Box 47, Miami, MO 65344. 816/886-7537

NORTH CAROLINA

Town Creek Indian Mound State Historic Site, Rte. 3 Box 50, Mount Gilead, NC 27306. 919/439-6802

OHIO

Campbell Mound, McKinley Ave., Columbus, OH.

Fort Ancient State Memorial, SR 350, Lebanon, OH. 513/932-4421

Fort Hill State Memorial, 13614 Ft. Hill Rd., Hillsboro, OH 45133. 513/588-3221

Great Mound, town cemetery, Marietta, OH.

Great Mound, Mound Avenue, Miamisburg, OH.

Moundbuilders Earthworks, SR 79, Newark, OH. 614/344-1920

Mound City Group National Monument, 16062 SR 104, Chillicothe, OH 45601. 614/774-1125

Octagon Earthworks, N. 33rd & Parkview Sts., Newark, OH.

Pyramid, town park, Marietta, OH.

Seip Mound, US 50, Bainbridge, OH.

Serpent Mound State Memorial, 3850 SR 73, Peebles, OH 45660. 513/587-2796

Story Mound, Delano Avenue, Chillicothe, OH.

Williamson Mound, US 42, Cedarville, OH.

Wright Earthworks, James & Waldo Sts., Newark, OH.

OKLAHOMA

Spiro Mounds Archaeological State Park, Rte. 2, Spiro, OK 74959. 918/962-2062

SOUTH CAROLINA

Fort Watson Mound Site, Santee National Wildlife Refugee, Rte. 2 Box 370, Summerton, SC 29148. 803/478-2217

TENNESSEE

Chucalissa Museum, Memphis State University, 1987 Indian Village Dr., Memphis, TN 38109. 901/785-3160

Old Stone Fort State Archaeological Park, Rte. 7 Box 7400, Manchester, TN 37355. 615/723-5073

Pinson Mounds State Archaeological Area, 460 Ozier Rd., Pinson, TN 38366. 901/988-5614

Shiloh National Military Park, P. O. Box 67, Shiloh, TN 38376. 901/689-5275

TEXAS

Caddoan Mounds State Historic Park, Rte. 2 Box 85C, Alto, TX 75925. 409/858-3218

WEST VIRGINIA

Grave Creek Mound State Park, Moundville, WV 26041. 304/843-1410

WISCONSIN

Aztalan State Park, c/o Glacial Drumlin State Trail, 1213 S. Main Street, Lake Mills, WI 53551. 414/648-8774

Lizard Mound County Park, Washington County Land Use and Park System, Rm. 150, 432 E. Washington St., West Bend, WI 53095. 414/335-4445

Roche-a-Cri State Park, Friendship Ranger Station, P.O. Box 100, Friendship, WI 53934. 608/339-3385

CANADA:

MANITOBA

Linear Mounds National Historic Site (near Melita), c/o Canadian Parks Service, 457 Main Street, Winnepeg, Manitoba R3B 3E8. 204/983-3179

ONTARIO

Serpent Mounds Provincial Park, Ontario. 705/295-6897

Southwold Earthworks, Point Pelee National Park, RR1, Leamington, Ontario N8H 3V4. 519/322-2365

A PARTICULARLY ELOQUENT legacy of ancient Native America is the collection of artifacts found in excavations of the earthworks. Many of these venerable objects from Ohio and Mississippi have been damaged to some degree, and though many have been photographed, few show details clearly.

The following line drawings of ancient Native American artifacts, with no claims to being fine art, are intended simply to provide accurate and cohesive images of the originals. Many of the designs, such as those scratched on shell, are even simpler. In this manner it was also possible to reconstruct missing or broken portions. Such instances are indicated in captions also providing, if known, the material, dimensions, period, site where found, and present location.

I. ANCIENT NATIVE AMERICAN PIPES

The tradition of pipes and smoking various natural substances began very early in Native America. In the Ohio period effigy pipes of the platform style, as in Figure 1, were predominant. The simpler bowl-and-stem style only appeared in later Mississippian times. The peoples of Ohio and Mississippi devoted much attention and skill to naturalistic detail and ornamentation of their pipes which were treasured possessions of a probably ceremonial nature.

This group of 20 pipes is a rare collection of pre-Columbian traditions in pipe-carving.

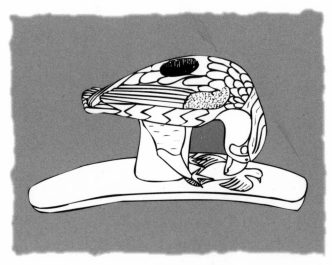

Fig. 1.

Fig. 1. FALCON EFFIGY PIPE
Stone, with river pearls for eyes
100 BC–AD 100, Ohio
Dimensions and location unknown

Part of the platform in front of the head is restored.

Fig. 2. SPOONBILL EFFIGY PIPE
Polished stone, dimensions unknown
100 BC–AD 100
Hopewell Mound, Ross County, Ohio
Field Museum of Natural History

Fig. 2.

Fig. 3.

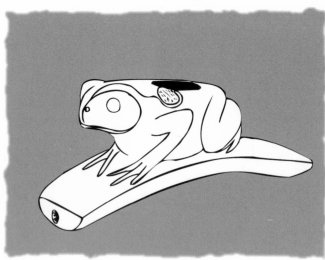

Fig. 4.

Fig. 5.

Fig. 6.

Fig. 3. BEAVER EFFIGY PIPE
Pipestone, river pearl, and bone
4.5 X 11.6 cm, AD 100-300
Bedford Mound, Pike County,
Illinois
Thomas Gilcrease Institute of American History and Art

The elegance of this piece suggests an import from the central Hopewell area.

Fig. 4. FROG EFFIGY PIPE
Stone, dimensions unknown
100 BC-AD 100
Mound City, Ross County, Ohio
Ohio Historical Society

Fig. 5. COYOTE EFFIGY PIPE
Catlinite, 6.4 X 7cm
100 BC-AD 100
Tremper Mound, Scioto County,
Ohio
Ohio Historical Society

Catlinite was obtained at the Pipestone (National Monument) quarry in southwestern Minnesota.

Fig. 6. LYNX EFFIGY PIPE
Red porphyry
100 BC-AD 100, Ohio
Dimensions and location unknown

Fig. 7. PANTHER EFFIGY PIPE
Steatite, 16 cm, AD 200-400
Mann site, Posey County, Indiana
Guennol Collection, on loan to The
Brooklyn Museum

Fig. 8. WINGED SHAMAN
EFFIGY PIPE
Greenstone, dimensions unknown
100 BC-AD 100, Ohio
The British Museum

Fig. 9. ADENA PIPE
Stone, 20 cm, 100 BC-AD 100
Adena Mound, Ross County, Ohio
Ohio Historical Society

Fig. 10. FROG EFFIGY PIPE
Bauxite, 13 X 16 X 10 cm
AD 1200 - 1400
Madison County, Illinois
Illinois State Museum

The Adena/Hopewell tradition of
pipe smoking carried over to the
Mississippian culture. This and following examples show a new flower-
ing of that art. The item held by the
frog is apparently a rattle.

Fig. 11. FELINE EFFIGY PIPE
Polished stone, 11.25 cm
AD 1200 - 1400
Moundville, Hale County, Alabama
Tennessee State Museum

Fig. 7.

Fig. 8.

Fig. 9.

Fig. 10.

Fig. 11.

Fig. 12.

Fig. 13.

Fig. 12. FELINE EFFIGY PIPE
Stone, 10.5 X 12.7 cm
AD 1200 - 1400
Anderson plantation, Chicot County,
Arkansas
Thomas Gilcrease Institute of American History and Art

Fig. 13. FALCON EFFIGY PIPE
Steatite, AD 1200 - 1400
Central Georgia
Dimensions and location unknown

Fig. 14.HUMAN EFFIGY PIPE
Polished bauxite, 20 cm
AD 1200 - 1400
Shiloh, Hardin County, Tennessee
Shiloh National Military Park
Museum

The Civil War battle of Shiloh was
fought on a mound site. The figure's
chipped nose is restored.

Fig. 15. HUMAN EFFIGY PIPE
Stone, 12.2 X 17 cm, ca. AD 1400
Emerald Site, Adams County,
Mississippi
The Brooklyn Museum

Fig. 14.

Fig. 15.

Fig. 16. HUMAN EFFIGY PIPE
Bauxite, 19.3 X 18 cm
AD 1200 - 1400
Piasa Creek Mound, Madison County, Illinois
Thomas Gilcrease Institute of American History and Art

The tassles on the shawl are more amorphous in the original.

Fig. 17. HUMAN EFFIGY PIPE
Stone, dimensions unknown
AD 1200 - 1400
Moundville, Hale County, Alabama
Heye Foundation, Museum of the American Indian

Fig. 18. WARRIOR EFFIGY PIPE
Stone, dimensions unknown
AD 1100 - 1250
Spiro, Le Flore County, Oklahoma
Heye Foundation, Museum of the American Indian

Fig. 19. CHUNKY PLAYER EFFIGY PIPE
Bauxite, 20.9 X 12.8 cm
AD 1200 - 1400
Muskogee County, Oklahoma
St. Louis Museum of Science and Natural History

In the game of chunky, spears were thrown at a rolling stone. It may also have had a divinatory function.

Fig. 20. HUMAN EFFIGY PIPE
Bauxite, 27.5 X 23 cm
AD 1100 - 1250
Spiro, Le Flore County, Oklahoma
The University Museum, University of Arkansas

Fig. 16.

Fig. 17.

Fig. 18.

Fig. 19.

Fig. 20.

Fig. 21.

Fig. 22.

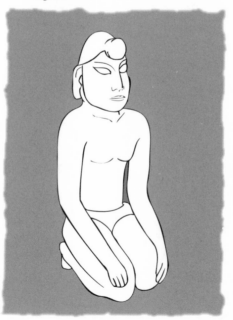

Fig. 23.

Fig. 24.

II. OTHER ANCIENT NATIVE AMERICAN FIGURES

The naturalistic details of small figurines from Ohio and Mississippi provide tantalizing images of these peoples and their ancient lifestyles. Some of them are funerary figures posed in virtually identical postures, indications of perhaps magical or religious significance.

Fig. 21. WRAY FIGURINE
Stone, dimensions unknown
100 BC - AD 100
Newark, Licking County, Ohio
Ohio Historical Society

The details of a bearskin and vessels suggest this figurine is a shaman.

Fig. 22. FIGURINE
Clay ceramic
AD 300 - 500, Missouri
Dimensions and location unknown

Perhaps a maize or harvest deity.

Fig. 23. FIGURINE - KNEELING MAN
Clay ceramic, 8.3 X 3.7 cm
100 BC - AD 100
Turner Mound, Hamilton County, Ohio
Peabody Museum of Archaeology and Ethnology

The original is cracked and chipped.

Fig. 24. FIGURINE - MOTHER AND CHILD
Clay ceramic, 100 BC - AD 100
Turner Mound, Hamilton County, Ohio
Dimensions and location unknown

The original is very cracked.

Fig. 25. MALE FIGURE
Stone, red and black paint, 46.2 cm
AD 1200 - 1400
Sellers Farm site, Wilson County,
Tennessee
Frank H. McClung Museum

Fig. 26. FEMALE FIGURE
Ceramic with paint, 20.3 cm
AD 1200 - 1400, Tennessee
Tennessee State Museum

Fig. 27. KELLER FIGURINE
Bauxite, 13 X 7 X 9.7 cm
AD 1200 - 1400
BBB Motor Site, Madison County,
Illinois
Illinois Archaeological Survey

The arms have been restored.

Fig. 28. PAIR OF HUMAN FIG-
URES
Marble, black and red paint, 61 cm
AD 1200 - 1400
Etowah, Bartow County, Georgia
Etowah Mounds Museum

The male figure's right knee and
hand have been restored.

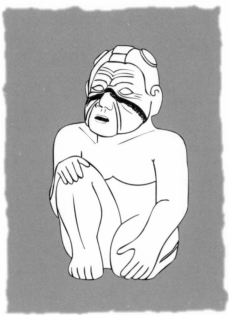

Fig. 25.

Fig. 26.

Fig. 27.

Fig. 28.

Fig. 29.

Fig. 30.

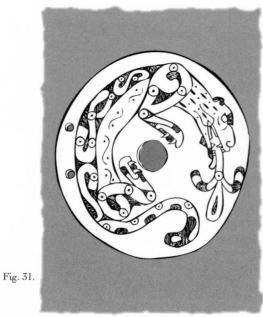

Fig. 31.

Fig. 32.

III. ANCIENT NATIVE AMERICAN GORGETS

The gorget, a large pendant perhaps worn on a cord, was a tradition continuing throughout the history of Native America. The use of seashell for this ornament testifies to far-flung trade routes. This group of 14 gorgets is again a rare collection of these remarkable images.

Fig. 29. SANDALSOLE GORGET
Marine shell, 19.4 X 7.2 cm
Red Ochre/Glacial Kame culture
1500 - 1000 BC, Great Lakes area
The Gordon Hart Collection

This earliest example is shaped like the sole of a sandal.

Fig. 30. CRAB ORCHARD SPRINGS GORGET
Inscribed marine shell
AD 100 - 300, Missouri
Dimensions and location unknown

In central Ohio, Hopewell tastes ran more to copper and mica ornaments, but gorgets were found in other areas. The drawing is dramatically corrected for symmetry.

Fig. 31. FAIRFIELD GORGET
Inscribed marine shell
AD 100 - 300, Missouri
Dimensions and location unknown

Fig. 32. WARRIOR GORGET
Inscribed marine shell, dimensions unknown, AD 1200 - 1400
Moundville, Hale County, Alabama
Heye Foundation, Museum of the American Indian

Fig. 33. CHUNKY PLAYER
GORGET
Inscribed marine shell, dimensions
unknown, AD 1200 - 1400
Eddyville, Lyon County, Kentucky
Smithsonian Institution

The implement in the figure's other
hand may be a mallet.

Fig. 34. CHUNKY PLAYER
GORGET
Inscribed marine shell
AD 1200 - 1400, Missouri
Dimensions and location unknown

The original is damaged around the
raised foot.

Fig. 35. DOUGLAS GORGET
Inscribed marine shell, 10.3 cm
diameter
AD 1200 - 1400, Missouri
American Museum of Natural
History

The attire of this figure is typical of
the so-called Southern Cult style
which spread across the Mississippian world in the thirteenth and four-
teenth centuries.

Fig. 36. WARRIOR GORGET
Inscribed marine shell, dimensions
unknown
AD 1200 - 1400, Tennessee
Heye Foundation, Museum of the
American Indian

This warrior is ornamented with the
Southern Cult bilobed arrow headdress, beaded forelock, apron pouch,
and ceremonial mace.

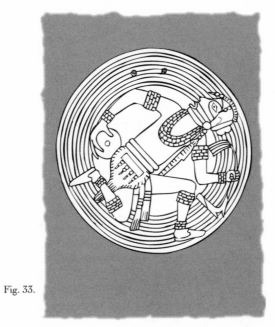

Fig. 33.

Fig. 34.

Fig. 35.

Fig. 36.

Fig. 37.

Fig. 38.

Fig. 39.

Fig. 40.

Fig. 41.

Fig. 42.

Fig. 37. FALCON WARRIOR GORGET
Cutout/inscribed marine shell, 14 cm diameter, AD 1200 - 1400
Etowah, Bartow County, Georgia
Etowah Mounds Museum

The Mississippian Falcon Warrior, an important element of the Southern Cult, may relate to the prominent Eagle Warrior of Meso-America.

Fig. 38. DOUBLE WARRIOR GORGET
Cutout/inscribed marine shell
11.5 cm diameter, AD 1200 - 1400
Hamilton County, Tennessee
Frank H. McClung Museum

These Falcon Warriors, by grasping a lock of the opponent's hair, are apparently counting coup.

Fig. 39. RACCOON DANCERS GORGET
Cutout/inscribed marine shell
17.9 cm diameter, AD 1100 - 1250
Spiro, Le Flore County, Oklahoma
Woolaroc Museum

The rattles and fans may indicate connections with the Southwest.

Fig. 40. SPIDER GORGET
Inscribed marine shell
AD 1200 - 1400, Illinois
Dimensions and location unknown

The spider was probably symbolic of the sun, as is the cross on its body.

Fig. 41. RATTLESNAKE GORGET
Inscribed marine shell
AD 1200 - 1400
McMahon Mound, Tennessee
Dimensions and location unknown

Fig. 42. WOODPECKER GORGET
Inscribed marine shell, dimensions unknown
AD 1200 - 1400, Tennessee
Frank H. McClung Museum

IV. SPECIAL RELICS OF OHIO

Fig. 43. BERLIN TABLET
Sandstone, 7.1 X 14.3 cm
100 BC - AD 100
Jackson County, Ohio
Ohio Historical Society

This bilobed tablet has identical bird motifs on both sides.

Fig. 44. WILMINGTON TABLET
Sandstone, 9.8 X 12.8 cm
100 BC - AD 100
Clinton County, Ohio
Ohio Historical Society

The complex designs could have some glyphic significance; the notches at the bottom may be calendar-related, given the apparent sun and moon at the top.

Fig. 45. ADENA TABLET
Stone, 100 BC - AD 100
Adena Mound, Ross County, Ohio
Dimensions and location unknown

Fig. 46. GRAVE CREEK TABLET
Stone, dimensions unknown
100 BC - AD 100
Moundville, Marshall County, West Virginia
Smithsonian Institution (but apparently lost)

There was much controversy about this tablet exhumed in 1838 from the Great Mound, mainly because the inscriptions were indecipherable. Recently these marks have been read as an ancient Iberian script used for words in Punic (Phoenician):
*"The mound raised-on-high for Tasach /
This tile / Queen caused-to-be-made."*

(See Reading List: Fell.)

Fig. S-47. CINCINNATI TABLET
Brown sandstone
100 BC - AD 100
Cincinnati, Hamilton County, Ohio
Dimensions and location unknown

Shown in a woodcut from Squier and Davis, this tablet included apparently floral motifs.

The reverse inscription has been guessed as many things, from simple marks made by sharpening tools to an impression of a manatee. However, in ancient Celtic Ogam, a script using combinations of strokes as letters, these marks are "b" and "l"—standard spelling for the name of the god Bel.

In discussions of transatlantic contacts with ancient America, the Grave Creek and Cincinnati tablets must be considered. So must another striking fact: the geometric earthworks and hillforts of Ohio closely coincide in time, shape, size, and probable function with earthworks raised in northern Europe by the ancient Celts.

Fig. 43.

Fig. 44.

Fig. 45.

Fig. S-47.

Fig. 46.

Fig. 48.

V. SPECIAL RELICS OF MISSISSIPPI

The Mississippians created a number of fantastic creatures, composites of serpent, bird, feline, human, and other species' characteristics. These Piasa monsters were surely mythological or mystical. (Among the Cherokee can be found a feline-headed winged serpent monster called the Uktena.)

Fig. 48. WINGED SERPENT
Detail, inscribed marine shell cup
AD 1100 - 1250
Spiro, Le Flore County, Oklahoma
Dimensions and location unknown

One of three interwoven serpents, this horned serpent, without the wings, could have originated in the Desert Southwest. The wings, however, ensure it is a Mississippian representation of the Meso-American plumed serpent (Quetzalcoatl).

Fig. 49. PIASA MONSTER
Detail, inscribed marine shell cup
AD 1100 - 1250
Spiro, Le Flore County, Oklahoma
Dimensions and location unknown

The original is very damaged. The bird and rattle-snake tails are restored. The head and headdress above the earspool and upper jaw are drawn from a detail on another cup.

Fig. 50. PICTOGRAPH —PIASA BIRD
Pictograph on limestone bluff, dimensions unknown
AD 1200 - 1400 (?)
Alton, Madison County, Illinois

The drawing is from a reconstructed pictograph seen by Pére Marquette in 1673. The original was observed by the priest-explorer on a bluff above the Mississippi River near Cahokia.

If the plumed serpent of Meso-America represented the union of earth (serpent) with sky (bird), the Piasa monster of the Mississippians, as a further evolution of that concept, may have symbolized the unity of all things, of all species and all realms of reality in the web of life on earth. This vision, an integral part of the Native American heritage, continues to offer very wise guidance to all peoples on the earth today.

Fig. 49.

Fig. 50.

▲▼

I. SITES AND CULTURES:

Barrett, S. A. Ancient Aztalan. Bulletin 13, Milwaukee Public Museum.

Brose, D. S. "An Historical and Archaeological Investigation of the Hopeton Earthworks," Report to the National Park Service (file GX-G115-6-0410), Midwest Archaeological Center, Lincoln, NE, 1976.

Brose, D. S., and Greber, N. Hopewell Archaeology. Kent State University Press, Kent, OH, 1979.

Buikstra, J. Hopewell in the Lower Illinois Valley. Scientific Paper No. 2, Archaeology Program, Northwestern University, Evanston, 1976.

Caldwell, J. R. and Hall, R. L., eds. Hopewellian Studies. Illinois State Museum, Scientific Papers, vol. 12, no. 3.

Caldwell, J. R., and Hall, R. L. Irene Mound Site, Chatham County, Georgia. University of Georgia Press, Athens, GA, 1941.

Carr, R. S. "Prehistoric Circular Earthworks in South Florida," Florida Anthropologist, vol. 38, 1985, pp. 288-301.

Chapman, C. H. The Archaeology of Missouri. University of Missouri Press, Columbia, 1980.

Coe, M.; Snow, D.; and Benson, E. Atlas of Ancient America. Facts on File Publications, NY, 1986.

Fowke, G. "Archaeological Investigations II." 44th Annual Report, Bureau of American Ethnology, 1926-27.

Fowler, M. L. Cahokia: Ancient Capital of the Midwest. Addison-Wesley Publishing, Menlo Park, CA, 1974.

Garbarino, M. S. Native American Heritage. Little, Brown, Boston, 1976.

Gibson, J. L. Poverty Point. Anthropological Study Series, No. 7, Louisiana Archeological Survey and Antiquities Commission, Baton Rouge, 1983.

Gilliland, M. S. The Material Culture of Key Marco, Florida. University Presses of Florida, Gainesville, 1975.

Greber, N. "Recent Excavations at the Edwin Harness Mound, Liberty Works, Ross County, Ohio," Kirtlandia 39, 1983.

Griffin, J. B., ed. Archaeology of the Eastern United States. University of Chicago Press, 1952.

Hudson, C. The Southeastern Indians. University of Tennessee Press, 1978.

Hyde, G. E. Indians of the Woodlands. University of Oklahoma Press, Norman, 1962.

Jennings, J. D. Prehistory of North America. McGraw-Hill, NY, 1974.

Jennings, J. D., ed. Ancient Native Americans. W. H. Freeman and Co., San Francisco, 1978.

Luer, G. M., and Almy, M. M. "Temple Mounds of the Tampa Bay Area," Florida Anthropologist, vol. 34, 1981, pp. 127-156.

McDonald, J. N., and Woodward, S. L. Indian Mounds of the Atlantic Coast, A Guide to Sites from Maine to Florida. McDonald and Woodward Publishing Co., Newark, Ohio, 1987.

Milanich, J. T. The Early Prehistoric Southeast: A Source Book. Garland Publishing, Inc., NY, 1985.

Moore, C. B. Certain Aboriginal Mounds of the Central Florida West Coast.

Moore, C. B. Certain Mounds of Arkansas and Mississippi.

Moore, C. B. Some Aboriginal Sites in Louisiana and Arkansas.

Moore, C. B. Some Aboriginal Sites on the Red River.

Moore, C. B. Certain Aboriginal Remains of the Black Warrior River. Journal of the Academy of Natural Sciences for Philadelphia, Philadelphia PA, 1905.

Moore, C. B. Moundville Revisited. Journal of the Academy of Natural Sciences for Philadelphia, Philadelphia PA, 1907.

Moorehead, W. K. Etowah Papers. Yale University Press, New Haven, CT, 1932.

Moorehead, W. K. Fort Ancient, Ohio. Robert Clarke & Co., Cincinnati, 1890.

Morse, D. F., and Morse, P. A. Archaeology of the Central Mississippi Valley. Academic Press, NY, 1983.

National Geographic Society. Mysteries of the Ancient World. Washington, DC, 1979.

Neuman, R. W., and Hawkins, N. W. Louisiana Prehistory. Anthropological Study Series, No. 6, Louisiana Archaeological Survey and Antiquities Commission, Baton Rouge, 1982.

Rowe, Chandler W. The Effigy Mound Culture of Wisconsin. Milwaukee Public Museum Publication in Anthropology, No. 3, 1956.

Schnell, F. T.; Knight, V. J. Jr.; and Schnell, G. S. Cemochechobee: Archaeology of a Mississippian Ceremonial Center on the Chattahoochee River. University of Florida Press, Gainesville, FL, 1981.

Seeman, M. F. The Hopewell Interaction Sphere: The Evidence for Interregional Trade and Structural Complexity. Indiana Historical Society, Prehistory Research Series, vol. 5, no. 2, 1979.

Sherrod, P., and Rolingson, M. A. Surveyors of the Ancient Mississippi Valley. Arkansas Archeological Survey Research Series, No. 28, Fayetteville, AR, 1987.

Shetrone, H. C. The Mound-Builders. Appleton-Century, NY, 1930.

Silverberg, R. Moundbuilders of Ancient America. New York Graphic Society, 1968.

Silverberg, R. The Mound Builders. Ohio University Press, Athens, 1986.

Smith, B., ed. Mississippian Settlement Patterns. Academic Press, NY, 1978.

Snow, D. The Archaeology of North America. Thames and Hudson, Ltd., London, 1976.

Squier, E. G., and Davis, E. H. Ancient Monuments of the Mississippi Valley. Smithsonian Contributions to Knowledge, vol. 1, NY, 1848.

Steponaitis, V. P. Ceramics, Chronology and Community Patterns, an Archaeological Study at Moundville. Academic Press, NY, 1983.

Thomas, C. "Burial Mounds of the Northern Sections of the United States," 5th Annual Report, Bureau of American Ethnology, 1883-84.

▲▼▲▼▲▼▲▼▲▼▲▼▲▼▲▼▲▼▲▼▲▼▲▼▲▼▲▼▲▼▲▼▲▼▲▼

Thomas, C. Catalogue of Prehistoric Works East of the Rocky Mountains. Bulletin 12, Bureau of American Ethnology, 1890.

Thomas, C. "Report on Mound Explorations." 12th Annual Report, Bureau of American Ethnology, 1890-91.

Trigger, B. G., ed. Native Shell Mounds of North America: Early Studies. Garland Publishing, Inc., NY, 1986.

Walker, W. M. The Troyville Mounds, Catahoula Parish, LA. Bulletin 113, Bureau of American Ethnology, 1936.

Walthall, J. A. Prehistoric Indians of the Southeast. University of Alabama Press, 1980.

Webb, W. S., and Baby, R. S.The Adena People, No. 2. Ohio Historical Society, Columbus, 1957.

Webb, W. S., and Snow, C. E. The Adena People. University of Tennessee Press, 1981.

Williamson, R. A., ed. Archaeoastronomy in the Americas. Ballena Press, Los Altos, CA, 1981.

Winchell, N. H. The Aborigines of Minnesota. Minnesota Historical Society, St. Paul, 1911.

II. ART OF ANCIENT AMERICA:

Atwater, C. "Description of the Antiquities Discovered in the State of Ohio and Other Western States," Archaeologia Americana: Transactions and Collections of the American Antiquarian Society, vol. 1, 1820, pp. 109-251.

Bierer, B. W. Indians and Artifacts in the Southeast. Bierer Publishing Co., Columbia, SC, 1980.

Brose, D. S.; Brown, J. A.; and Penney, D. W. Ancient Art of the American Woodland Indians, Harry N. Abrams, Inc., Publishers, NY, 1985.

Coe, R. T. Sacred Circles, Two Thousand Years of North American Indian Art. Catalogue of Exhibition, Nelson Gallery of Art, Atkins Museum of Fine Arts, Kansas City MO, 1977.

Dickens, R. S., Jr. Of Sky and Earth, Art of the Early Southeastern Indians. Catalogue of Exhibition, The High Museum of Art, Atlanta, GA, 1982.

Holmes, W. H. "Art in Shell of the Ancient Americans," 2nd Annual Report, Bureau of American Ethnology, 1881.

Jones, C. C., Jr. Antiquities of the Southern Indians, Particularly of the Georgia Tribes. D. Appleton and Co., NY, 1873.

Moorehead, W. K. Prehistoric Relics. Andover Press, Andover MA, 1905.

Phillips, P., and Brown, J. A. Pre-Columbian Shell Engravings from the Craig Mound at Spiro, OK. Peabody Museum Press, Cambridge, MA, 1978.

III. FOR MORE INFORMATION ON:

A. The El Paraíso civilization in South America:

Engel, F. A. An Ancient World Preserved. Crown Publishers, NY, 1976.

B. Transoceanic contacts with ancient Native America:

Fell, B. America B. C. Demeter Press, NY, 1976.

Shao, P. The Origin of Ancient American Cultures. Iowa State University Press, Ames, 1983.

C. The earliest records of European contacts with Mississippi:

de la Vega, G. The Florida of the Inca. University of Texas Press, Austin, 1951.

Elvas, Gentleman of. Narratives of the Career of Hernando de Soto. Reprint edition, Palmetto Books, Gainesville, FL, 1968.

Laudonnière, René Goulaine de. L'Histoire notable de la Floride. Paris, 1586.

Le Challeux, Nicholas. Discours de l'histoire de la Floride. Dieppe, 1566.

Le Moyne de Morgues, Jacques. Narrative of Le Moyne. Boston, 1875.

Lorant, S., ed. The New World, The First Pictures of America. Duell, Sloan & Pearce, NY, 1946.

Ribaut, Jean. The Whole & True Discouerye of Terra Florida. Facsimile edition. University of Florida Press, Gainesville, FL, 1964.